IN PURSUIT
OF COLERIDGE

Some of the Notebooks being rebound.

IN PURSUIT
OF COLERIDGE

KATHLEEN COBURN

THE BODLEY HEAD
LONDON SYDNEY
TORONTO

ACKNOWLEDGMENTS

The author is grateful to The Literary Trustees of Walter de la Mare, and The Society of Authors as their representative, for permission to quote from his poem 'The Bards'; to Times Newspapers Ltd for permission to quote from the article 'Notebooks of Coleridge' which appeared in *The Times* on 28th July, 1951; and to Routledge & Kegan Paul Ltd and Princeton University Press for permission to reproduce as the frontispiece to this volume a photograph of the notebooks taken from Volume 1 of *The Notebooks of Samuel Taylor Coleridge*.

© Kathleen Coburn 1977
ISBN 0 370 30002 5
Printed and bound in Great Britain for
The Bodley Head Ltd
9 Bow Street, London WC2E 7AL
by W & J Mackay Ltd, Chatham
Set in 'Monotype' Imprint
First published 1977

CONTENTS

IN PURSUIT
OF COLERIDGE

PROLOGUE

I am often asked how and when I happened to become interested in Coleridge, and so I preface this tale of the pursuit with a few facts about personal origins, for whatever portents anyone chooses to see there.

I am a fourth-generation Canadian of Scots-Irish pioneer stock, some of whom left Antrim, Sligo, and County Down, to escape the nineteenth-century potato famine; some earlier. All were Protestants and dissenters from Anglicanism, with their faces set against any establishment in Canada, ecclesiastical, political, or social. Nevertheless, a sense of a rich heritage from the past, and the need of its nourishment for our Canadian roots, was strong with us always. I am irredeemably Canadian and have never pined as some of my contemporaries do (or did) to have an English accent.

My father, after a theological course in Victoria College in the University of Toronto, became a Methodist minister in Ontario. His Belfast-educated father before him, though blind, was a saddleback lay-preacher with the sense to marry a capable woman of log-cabin stock who managed to bring up a son and three daughters on no money at all. My father emulated him in this also. They both had a spontaneous natural eloquence and an Irish love of language.

We were a family of six children, four boys and two girls, of which I was one of the happy middles—less burdened by responsibilities than the two elder, and more free-wheeling than two bespectacled younger ones. Being a member of a large family was a factor in life of which I was always conscious, more pleasantly perhaps in retrospect as the light mellows with the years. We all read widely, without much guidance. However, the family conversation, though very vigorous and opinionated, was not often literary; the Bible, it is true, was read into our bones every night at the supper table when we had evening prayers. Though very sure that parental authority was unanimous, and based on firm principles and affection, in general we were lightly directed. As children, often argumentative and even quarrelsome, we yet rallied in unity against outside attack on any one of us. Somehow competition was discouraged; it certainly aroused no adult interest. Praise and blame were equally infrequent. I felt on the whole—within the basic principles of truthfulness, fair play, and so on—free in my own world. I think this was an unusual piece of luck in the type of fervent Methodist *milieu* of that period.

The Puritan emphasis on moral values was certainly not stinted. No man was an island, nor any woman or child either, and every one must be prepared to be his brother's keeper—always mindful of Mother's insistence on a decent sense of privacy. Father's Christianity was essentially practical, not in the least mystical nor even very theological; for him the good tidings meant the good life, physical as well as spiritual, for every human being in the world, and the Church was useless if it did not fight against social evils on every level. He was a pioneer, sometimes as comical as he was courageous, in righting various social wrongs in Canada. For me personally life was, I suppose, a bit pinched—not many luxuries— but it was easy and free-flowing; the stream seemed with me, not against me.

In the hot summer months, one glorious release from the dingy city parsonages of those days was the life in a summer cottage on an uninhabited shore of Lake Joseph. It was provided by a better-off uncle who taught us as children to swim, to find our way in the bush by compass and trail-blazing, to paddle a canoe, to fish slap-happily; in short, to be aware of animal, mineral and vegetable, and all the pleasures large and small of rocks, water, woods and sun. It was there Gran taught me at the age of nine how to swing an axe, a great enjoyment to this day. Her country skills and knowledge gave us a continuity with the pioneer past, delicious through her savouring of it. Was it her independent spirit that encouraged in me a healthy taste for solitary wanderings, quiet moments of sensing the pulsations of earth? However it was, the sunshine filtered through those days as it did through the branches of the forest trees. Coleridge refers in a notebook entry to those happy feelings of childhood 'when summer days appeared twenty times as long'.

Naturally it was always a painful wrench to leave this natural world to go back to school, too often an unknown school, as Methodist parsons in those days were frequently shifted. Those co-educational day schools wherever we happened to live did not inspire, neither did they harass me. Up to the end of the four undergraduate years in an honour course in the University of Toronto I could never decide upon a profession, although I always supposed I should find one, or that it would find me. I naturally expected to earn my own living, and had serious thoughts of medicine (but no funds) or biology. I was fearful of becoming a school teacher, I knew that. And one negative consequence of being brought up in a large family in parsonage poverty was the conviction in early adolescence that nothing would induce me to be a parson's wife or the mother of a large family. All that washing and ironing and mending! All that cooking and dusting! Perhaps something was unconsciously conveyed to me of my mother's suppressed craving for a few oases of peace and pleasure. In any event, I did not worry about what would become of me, and no one forced me into firmness of mind about any goal.

It was not the most likely terrain to produce literary harvests— still less the whirl of excitements that came with them.

In the first place, why Coleridge? To the romantic poets in general I was drawn first, no doubt, by a good teacher—my first real teacher of English. Pelham Edgar's unaggressive fervour in reciting them aloud made his readings an experience. Such poems —I think of Wordsworth and the *Lucy* poems as well as *The Prelude*, of Keats's *La Belle Dame sans Merci* as well as the great Odes, of Shelley's *West Wind* and *Prometheus Unbound*, of Coleridge's *Frost at Midnight* and *Dejection*, not to mention 'The old Navigator' as he called him—such poems offered a moving and elegant extension of life beyond the confines of Ontario. Looking back I see, too, that Wordsworth and Coleridge especially carried powerfully into poetry those intense satisfactions from earth, sun, and water which can be built into one in Canada by these elements. Their poems not only enhanced these pleasures but somehow justified them to the Puritan ethos, by attending at the same time to 'the still sad music of humanity'. They also, for another thing, led one back to a remoter, more expansive, more secure past, to the seventeenth-century poets they admired, back beyond the Canadian frontiers, beyond the industrial revolution, beyond John Wesley and the eighteenth century, into a more lyrical world.

And to Shakespeare. Coleridge gave me a more comprehensible, more deeply personal Shakespeare.

'What is *Lear*?—It is storm and tempest—the thunder at first grumbling in the far horizon, then gathering around us, and at length bursting in fury over our heads,—succeeded by a breaking of the clouds for a while, a last flash of lightning, the closing in of night, and the single hope of darkness! And *Romeo and Juliet?*— It is a spring day, gusty and beautiful in the morn, and closing like an April evening with the song of the nightingale;—whilst *Macbeth* is deep and earthy—composed to the subterranean music of a troubled conscience, which converts every thing into the wild and fearful!'

Of all the English romantics, Coleridge had the keenest interest in philosophy. The first whiff of that, especially when it showed a psychological bent, fairly pulled me along, through bafflement, slave labour, and despair. And still does.

From all these causes—they were certainly not fully apparent reasons at the time—I pelted headlong after Coleridge.

But it is difficult to credit the extensive ignorance with which one set out in the late nineteen-twenties. That Coleridge of all English critics best taught us how to understand not only Shakespeare but the Bible; that he was excited by public affairs and wrote powerfully as a journalist against slavery of all kinds—of children in the cotton factories, as well as slaves in the sugar plantations; that he was devoted to the principle of freedom of mind—in the legislature, in the press, in the classroom—these things coming into view from time to time stimulated the pursuit. I came to appreciate his personal classlessness in comparison with the snobbish Toryism of Wordsworth or Scott or the twisted limited Toryism of Southey. I had not known that he was one of the first English climbers in the Lake District, that he was a far more energetic walker than Wordsworth in spite of the debilitating bondage to opium, still less that his determination and effort to see the other side of the mountain were as characteristic of his walks as of his intellectual life. Max Beerbohm's amusing cartoon 'Coleridge Table Talking' concealed the fact that the talk was on every subject under the sun—and that Coleridge mostly knew what he was talking about. The newest developments in chemistry, as well as the alchemists; Homer, Paracelsus, Vico as well as Kant and the Kantians; children; economic matters like the paper-money controversy or the depressive consequences of the Napoleonic wars; witchery, mesmerism, the analysis of dreams, population, and prices; love, how different from friendship. He emerged as more practical than poets and philosophers are reputed to be. Had he not been for a year and a half in Malta second in importance to the British High Commissioner during the Napoleonic wars? Like Noël Coward he took the journey to try to get rid of his neuroses—only to find that the neuroses followed him, as Coward put it, 'on the next boat'. But through all his emotional difficulties Coleridge came to understand a great deal about the complexities and contradictions of the human condition. At every turn he questioned—questioned—and questioned his questions.

One did not know these things then, partly because so much of Coleridge was not in print. Of that I had not the faintest notion either. And the prose that had been published—except for the *Biographia Literaria*, 'the best book of literary criticism in English and the most annoying book in any language', someone called it—was available only secondhand in nineteenth-century editions.

I suppose an undergraduate in my shoes in England would have been told more about the prose works, about materials in the British Museum, and might have speculated about surviving papers in the hands of the distinguished family that bears his name. But I did not know of the small sheaves of manuscripts in the Museum, nor of the great-grandson who had a few notebooks and a few hundred printed books from Coleridge's library; they had come down through Coleridge's son, Derwent, to his son Ernest Hartley Coleridge, and thus to the Reverend Gerard Coleridge of Leatherhead. Nor did I dream of the still larger hoard (of which but a very few people knew enough to dream) of some fifty-five notebooks, assorted other manuscripts and annotated books in Ottery St Mary, owned then by Geoffrey Lord Coleridge, the third baron and grandson of the Lord Chief Justice Coleridge, great, great, great nephew of STC. All this was to emerge with incredible rapidity once I got to England two years after graduation.

What I was totally unprepared for, above all, was the degree to which I should find myself deeply wrenched by the thoughts and sensibilities and imaginative projections of 'mighty poets in their misery dead'—dead but incredibly alive in my own time—the sort of discovery that leaves even a brash undergraduate 'silent, upon a peak in Darien'.

But when the first question about Coleridge—a mere snowflake of a question—drifted into my head, I had no notion of any of this. Nor had I any ambitions for a post-graduate university career. We had no professors in the family circle, no talk of old books or manuscripts, nor could I have imagined myself having the patience for close literary research.

Something, no doubt, came from the genes, my mother's genes. Her experience taught her, and told us, that 'things usually turn out for the best, dear'. And so they seemed to do for me at every turn in the road. I never consciously tried to compete in any way, just stumbled upon one likely-looking opportunity after another and enjoyed pursuing each one as it came. The story of tracking Coleridge is one of almost uninterrupted good luck. Very early in the quest for whatever it was, somehow to do with Coleridge, I began to feel myself a mere instrument in an unfolding of events, and the deepest pleasure was in being the instrument. Things simply of themselves turned sweet, not sour. The snowflake was turning steadily into a large rolling snowball.

Yet I suppose I did have something to do with it at the start. It would be disingenuous to deny it. Hamlet at a critical moment in his life uttered my favourite statement in all Shakespeare: 'The readiness is all.' I suppose you could say that from obscure causes I must have been to some extent ready—at least to ask a question, to see a break in the trees. And behold, there were the 'caverns, measureless to man',

> 'And there were gardens bright with sinuous rills,
> Where blossomed many an incense-bearing tree.
> And here were forests ancient as the hills,
> Enfolding sunny spots of greenery.'

But heaven only knows what readiness is, or what prepares it. Perhaps the weather. All our Canadian weathers! The necessity to adapt to extreme change is at least part of the stimulus of the northness of Canada; it may have something to do with that resourcefulness for which I believe Canadians have some reputation. Certainly the bold beauty of the Great Lakes landscape in which I grew up encourages adventure. Perhaps paramount, abounding physical health and strength gave zest to the taste, touch, sight, sound, and smell of it all.

PROLOGUE

However it was, this book aims to tell the story of one particular pursuit. It is not an autobiography. It omits much of life that has been rich in other kinds of personal rewards. This is about one series of adventures that began quite blindly. Then a succession of fortunate disappointments, lucky mishaps, and witless choices of forks in the road developed unexpected centrifugal force and flung me out to new horizons.

I

1928–1935

The first nudge in the Coleridge direction was given to me in a classroom in Victoria College, my father's old Methodist college in the University of Toronto.

In the spring of 1928, in what used to be Room 14 in the south-west corner of the ground floor, Pelham Edgar gave nine-o'clock lectures on English Romantic poetry to his fourth-year students. He was the Head of the English department (no mere Chairman in those days), a gifted gentleman who read poetry with gusto and respect, and taught other people to write better than the frustrations of his life permitted him to write himself. If the English department in Victoria College has an enviable reputation for freedom, various-ness, and harmony, it is largely owing to this man. I arrived late for his lecture one morning, and to my embarrassment he was reading aloud as I entered the room an essay of mine on Wordsworth. He didn't lift his eyes, but it was typical of him that after class he should stop me to say, nervously chewing his moustache, 'That Wordsworth essay—it *was* good you know—sorry to hear your mother is so ill—heavy duties for you and all that—don't feel you must come to these nine o'clocks. Use the library—better use of your time.' But fortunately I did not always accept this humane advice, for a few lectures later he introduced us to Coleridge's *Biographia Literaria*, John Livingston Lowes's *Road to Xanadu* (just published) and to the whole business of the imagination, for me a first glimmering notion, the first articulation of something felt but never before expressed. A turning point.

Coleridge was not a pet subject with Pelham Edgar, but a good one, for Edgar immensely respected a true poet and was well aware that in 1928 Coleridge was neglected. At that time Coleridge was usually tagged on as an academic afterthought to Wordsworth and insufficiently regarded as an imagination active in a broad spectrum of human interests—philosophy, psychology, chemistry, education, theology, politics and economics and much else. Edgar, moved by the thought of Coleridge's personal as well as intellectual problems, hit hard at Coleridge's nineteenth-century detractors, 'lesser minds unfit to tie the laces of his shoes,' he said. Edgar set up currents in the mind that were not specifically but only suggestively in his words, such was his gift as a teacher. He had disturbed my comfortable nine-o'clock doze by starting in my mind a few vague questions about the possibilities of links between Coleridge and the German philosophers we had been reading with G.S. Brett two or three weeks before. Brett, Professor of Philosophy and at this time Dean of the Graduate School in the University of Toronto, had written a three-volume *History of Psychology*, and was more intensely interested than some historians of ideas in the functioning of the imagination. He therefore was deeply attracted to the Romantic poets. Loved by his students, with his wide classical erudition he was somewhat feared by his colleagues in other departments, especially English. So far as I was concerned, two good teachers unknowingly were rubbing sticks together that smouldered into a little flame in the damp leaves of an immature undergraduate head. Out of total ignorance came an excitement and a curiosity that forty-five years and more have not quenched—nor indeed satisfied.

Brett had conceived for Toronto a course in Philosophy, English and History, rather like Oxford's Modern Greats but substituting English for economics. It was a rich and fairly heavy dish planned for hard workers, students with a philosophical bent but suffering from the meagre Ontario schooling in classical languages; it confronted one with a wide range of reading based on specific texts from the pre-Socratics (in translation) onwards. In the fourth year one was reading nineteenth-century philosophy, chiefly English and German, nineteenth-century political and social history, and the English literature of the same period. Perhaps my first bit of good luck was to have been born before such spacious and planned honour courses went out of existence in the University of Toronto. 'PE and H' might have been designed to create Coleridgians; without it I wonder if for me there would have been the least starting flicker of a flame.

Nor would the little blaze have burned so long had not Victoria College, by offering a small teaching scholarship, made postgraduate work a possibility. Victoria has generally lived up to its non-conformist principles by tolerating happily those in its midst who do not conform to it. After the results of the degree examinations were known, Pelham Edgar rang up from his golf club.

'I say, old thing,' said he in his shyly casual way, 'I hear you don't think much of how we treat essays in the Victoria English department?' An unintelligible splutter was my miserable answer, recollecting as I did my protest to Ned Pratt, the poet and senior member of the department (with whom Pelham Edgar was undoubtedly playing golf that day), that no essay of mine had ever been adequately torn to shreds. Edgar enjoyed but took pity on my confusion.

'Well, all I want to say is, I am sorry about that—but how would you like to come and try reading a few essays for us yourself next year? I could offer you a very small sum, miserable pittance—very poor—but may be you could live in, as a don—and do some post-graduate work too?'

So gently did he offer direction and help. In 1928—just before the Crash—jobs dangled dangerously from every tree, but I was bewildered and uncertain; here was a year or two of treading water. I could do an MA that would cut across my dual interest, in English literature and philosophy, and remain (so I thought) un-committed.

The catch was that no one in the English department was prepared to take on a thesis dealing with Coleridge's philosophical ideas. Would I not switch to Wordsworth? The secretary suggested that plenty of people could help me there. Wordsworth I enjoyed deeply, I said, but my curiosity had to do with Coleridge. Brett cut the Gordian knot and appeared sardonically to relish the discomfort of the English department by offering to supervise me himself; as Dean of the Graduate School he could hardly be turned down by the English department.

'What will you call it?—"Philosophical Tendencies in Coleridge", or some such title? Something of a sort to give you scope?' We were conspirators without any illusions about such theses being 'a contribution to knowledge'; we knew this one was to be useful only to me.

Apart from the excitement of reading Coleridge right through for the first time, the post-graduate years in Toronto, and later in Oxford, were altogether full of good fortune. A casual coincidence in 1929 presented the possibility of applying for an overseas scholarship. This in 1930 was something not at all to be taken for granted. The few Canadian students who went abroad on scholarships large enough to take care of ocean passages and a year in a college for post-graduate study were mostly science students, and male. For women there was the Federation of University Women's Senior Travelling Scholarship, open to all Canada, twelve hundred dollars, even then not enough on which to pinch by; and one other, open to both men and women, the Imperial Order of the Daughters of the Empire War Memorial Scholarships, one for each province, worth eighteen hundred dollars. As another happy chance and a word of gratitude to a true friend, I must record that if one of the other applicants for the scholarship, Alice Muckle, had not pestered me about submitting my application by the due date, she might have gone abroad instead of me.

These I.O.D.E. scholarships were for a year only, and at that time rarely renewed. A misunderstanding with some of the scholarship committee about its policy of non-renewal was cause me to embarrassment at the end of my first year in Oxford, and made it necessary for me to borrow the entire sum for the second year and for the long vacation in between. It is not being Pollyana to say, although it is no argument for the policy (which has since been improved upon), that this, too, turned out for the best. The oblique advantages were that the *contretemps* compelled me to cover my debt by taking out an insurance policy which became very useful later.

So it was Oxford. I had innocently applied to Trinity College, Dublin, only to be told firmly by the authorities there that they did not admit women to post-graduate studies. Deplorable, but not the last time fate was frustrating my wishes for my own good.

Oxford, dreaming spires and all, was more or less as fantasy had pictured it—except for the damp October cold, and the high voices of female undergraduates. Never was a Canadian winter so bone-chilling as that first one in Oxford—and never voices so shrill as those of English girls fresh from their public schools. They were ridiculously mature-sounding to Canadian ears; we associated those voices somehow with the mature English women who as wives and mothers had migrated to Canada. They made three of us, all freshers together at St Hugh's, laugh stupidly among ourselves until we got used to them. The dining-room the first night was a nightmare of sound—not only to Canadians—the decibels outrageously high for the relatively low ceiling of a women's college hall. How should we ever survive that din every night? It was never so bad after the first dinner, but the high loud hum in hall is one of the characteristic sounds of an Oxford women's college that no one who has lived with it could ever fail to remember.

St Hugh's was friendly. In spite of the noise and of having one of the least attractive rooms, I still enjoy in memory the sensation of that very first night, of settling into an armchair at my fire and sensing in some serene way that childhood was at last over and adult life had begun. From my windows only roof-tops and a night sky full of stars were to be seen.

> 'The moving Moon went up the sky,
> And nowhere did abide,
> Softly she was going up,
> And a star or two beside—'

The Mariner projected his own feelings enviously towards the stars, I more happily.

'In his loneliness and fixedness he yearneth towards the journeying Moon, and the stars that still sojurn, yet still move onward; and every where the blue sky belongs to them, and is their appointed rest, and their native country and their own natural homes, which they enter unannounced, as lords that are certainly expected, and yet there is a silent joy at their arrival.' The silent joy was mine.

Painfully aware of the great gaping chasms in my English reading, I expected to read for Schools—that is, as we should put it, to take the undergraduate course in English. At the first tutorial interview, however, Ethel Seaton urged me, after some searching questions, to think again.

'You are already too badly bitten by Coleridge to accept the amount of Anglo-Saxon required of undergraduates,' she said, 'and you are evidently longing to strike out on your own. Find a Coleridge thesis topic and let us discuss it. Take your time, but register for the B. Litt.' I still hankered for the weekly tutorial experience of Schools and I was full of anxiety and guilt about my undergraduate gaps, but I knew she was right. It was life-saving to

have her say so, unequivocally. Had I, by going to Dublin or even
to another Oxford college, missed her good advice, the consequent
floundering and frustration could have been serious.

Miss Seaton was a surprise packet. The exterior was the very
model of a model Oxford don of the generation of English women
who first fought their way through Oxford and Cambridge; she
was a little younger than the very first of these, but in dress and
manner she seemed to belong with their mothers. She had the
sallow skin and dry mouse-coloured hair of the burner of the midnight oil, and she wore her navy blue serge skirts very long, to
the ankle, when the rest of us wore ours somewhere rather less
far below the knee. Her rather high voice could be severe! The
shelves all around her study bulged books, two and more deep, so
that sometimes there was some digging for them; they also sat
horizontally, wedged in between the tops of others and the next
shelf, and in piles everywhere, sometimes with paper jackets on,
sometimes not, more often than not with untidy slips of paper in
them, scruffy, or spanking fresh. Books were tools rather than
treasured objects, her tools for teaching chiefly. She cared intensely
about the success of her students and worried about their compe-
tence and their working habits. I never had a formal tutorial from
her, for in my post-graduate studies she was, as she made clear,
only my 'moral tutor', a liaison between me and the college, not my
supervisor; she was to keep track of me in a general way. She
interpreted her function towards me most generously, recognizing
my needs: she screwed me down to the first year B.Litt examinations, at the dryness of which I was inclined to baulk, and made me
work at the technicalities of Chaucer texts, English secretary hand,
bibliographical problems I didn't care a hoot about, and the history
of English studies, never bullying me into the view that I *ought* to
know these things, but only making sure I got through those tiresome examinations. She was secretly as keen on my Coleridge work
as I was but more realistic about the required preliminaries.

She was a surprise packet, for the primness concealed a love of
hilarity, whether it was about fourteenth-century scribes, Shakespeare's hand in the play *Sir Thomas More*, Gilbert and Sullivan
(she took me to *Ruddigore*), Sir Edmund Chambers's squeaky tan
boots, or—as the years went on—my latest Coleridge find. She was
herself a doughty researcher, but beset by luck almost as bad as my

own was good. She once said, speaking of the exacting slavery side of it, 'You go to a strange city or town where you know no one, you sleep at your own expense in a strange bed, and you spend three weeks combing lists in filthy dusty records of births, marriages, and deaths, and in the end it all boils down to a line and a half of small print in a footnote: "This name does not occur in the fifty-four parish registers of Southampton"!' She envied me the fact that Coleridge required no such tedious searching of parish registers. 'But you, my dear Miss Coburn,' she said, 'were born, if not with a silver spoon in your mouth, at least with a manuscript in your cradle.' But that was two decades farther along the road.

Long after I went down from Oxford and came to know her better, and only then, did Miss Seaton begin to call me Kathleen. Through our occasional meetings over many years it was always the same: we always laughed as if life became absurd the moment we met. Even after she became ill and almost immobile, she was still chuckling over herself as my 'erstwhile moral tutor', an ambiguity I once had the temerity to perpetrate in a Gaudy dinner speech. Yet, for all her gaiety, she must have suffered as one of a generation that hesitated to give or receive expressions of affection. When I ventured for the first time to kiss her goodbye, though she smiled sweetly, her large blue eyes filled with tears. On one of my departures for home when she was very frail indeed, she made herself say, 'Don't leave it too long to come again.' I visited her on every trip to England and now alas, I shall not do so again.

To return to our first meeting, and her insistence on a B. Litt. The B. Litt. procedure took two years: one to provide training and background for research—the history of English studies with David Nichol Smith, textual criticism with Percy Simpson, bibliography with Strickland Gibson, and biographical materials with E. K. Chambers—the second year to be free for the writing of a thesis under a supervisor. The names of the lecturers are impressive and some of the work was useful, notably Strickland Gibson's classes in bibliography—he was later to become a sub-librarian at Bodley—but the whole course was less well planned then than it is now, and much of it was dull and, to me, tedious. Nor did Oxford find it any easier than Toronto to provide a supervisor interested in and knowledgeable about Coleridge's thought. The person *faute de mieux* finally victimised by the Board of Studies smiled on me and did his best to be kind, but Coleridge was not the meat for the editor of Peacock, and Brett Smith's invitations to tea twice a term were a strained though amiable formality. By great good fortune my first year in Oxford coincided with John Livingston Lowes's visiting lectureship, in the second term of which he talked about Coleridge, Wordsworth, Keats, and Shelley. He lectured to crowded rooms in the Schools, with people sitting on window ledges and on the floor outside the door—the only lectures I heard in the Oxford of 1930–32 that were really exciting.

What Oxford provided was not instruction. Nor was it only the opportunity for work, leisure, books, and talk. Rather it gave an assured sense of the value of a real knowledge of the past (as distinct from a mere sentiment for it), a revelation of the essential interplay in the scholar's life between high seriousness and lively pleasures. Of such is the happiness of learning.

In the first Oxford term, another most crucial happy accident in the long series of happy accidents helped to beat down the limitations of provinciality and inexperience. It came from going to a party I very nearly skipped. Lady Frances Ryder was having one of her receptions at Rhodes House for all visiting 'colonial' scholars, a continuation of her organized hospitality for troops during the first war. (People then were still using the word 'colonial' for Canadians, though with some embarrassed floundering for a substitute.) At the last moment I wanted to back out of the party. It was a wet night, which meant the expense of a taxi (evening skirts were long), and there had just arrived a Coleridge book I was longing to read. The other Canadians badgered me into going.

A number of Oxford hostesses were assisting Lady Frances, and in one of those circular games I found myself sitting with a silent young man on my right and a Mrs Boyle on my left. When to my right all my small stock of conversational ploys were exhausted on the shy gentleman whose replies were restricted to 'Yes' and 'No', it became evident that she too was in the same trouble with a similarly monosyllabic young man on her left. She turned her bright blue seventy-year-old eyes on me and said cheerfully, 'Let's give up and just enjoy ourselves!' We did. She was full of tales about various people of importance in the room, a vigorous lady determined to do her duty but equally determined not to be bored by it. At the end of the evening, with all her mischievous charm

and kindness she suddenly said, 'I have two *dreadful* women coming to lunch next Monday. Won't you come and help? They *are*
dreadful. *Do* come. I live at Great Milton—the house from which
Fairfax besieged Oxford, and from which Milton is said to have
courted his first wife, Mary Powell. I have a few interesting things
to show you. You could bike out?'

She had typically understated the beauty and interest of her
house, but, in a way, fortunately enough, not the appalling un-
pleasantness of her guests. She showed them some association
items in glass cases in the drawing-room, and in the garden after
lunch signalled to me to stay behind after they went. 'I have many
more interesting things upstairs,' she said *sotto voce*. So it was that
we had some time alone together in the course of which she asked
about my work. When I said 'Coleridge' she looked out into space
a minute and smiled, a little wickedly perhaps, or so it seemed in
retrospect. 'Would you care to have an introduction to the family?
I think I could arrange it.' For that question I was quite unprepared, but even in a green condition of total ignorance about
what family there was or what papers they might have, I knew that
I was being offered something important. The reasons why could
take their course.

She suggested that for part of the Christmas vacation I should
go to Sidmouth, on the Devon coast four miles south of Ottery St
Mary. Ottery St Mary! There really was music in the very name,
and it had special resonances for me. It was *his* birthplace, and
against better reason there was magic around it too. To be heading
straight as a die for it in the first Oxford vacation was electrifying,
incredible to a very young, very starry-eyed, very ebullient bore.
Anyhow Ottery! There the introduction would somehow be
effected. A telegram from her arrived, forwarded from college—
what was my address in Sidmouth? How stupidly careless I had
been, yet Mrs Boyle, accustomed to the heedless and wild young,
had persisted in her effort to find me. A few days later came an
invitation to lunch at the Chanter's House; Lady Coleridge would
meet me at the bus stop.

To the end of memory I shall see her there, in her blue and
white cotton housedress, a cardigan over her shoulders, peering
with apprehension but also expectancy, timid yet amused, gentle,
concerned yet welcoming, beautiful; there were signs of a more

youthful kind of beauty once upon a time, but there was absolutely
no self-consciousness of it in her now. Her large, heavy maternal
hands moved a bit nervously. A short walk up the hill led not to the
old vicarage where Coleridge was born—that had burned down—
but never mind, this was the soft South Devon air, these were the
cobbled streets and here was the beautiful church of his childhood.
The church really must be one of the loveliest in England, a small
model in warm slightly rosy stone for Exeter Cathedral, and as we
stood chattering about its beauty the bells began to ring, 'the poor
man's only music' that Coleridge remembered from his childhood.
A moment for sentiment. Why not?

A little gate took us into the garden of the Chanter's House. The
garden—lawns, oaks, a yew-tree walk, a goldfish pond—was
bounded on one side by the house and a red brick wall; on the other
side it stretched down to hay fields and pasture-land. First impressions of the house were of a Keble College type of stripey
bacon brick monster but mellowed, more friendly than awe-
inspiring, clearly a nineteenth-century transformation of an old
manor house, details of which I was to learn later. The original
house had been built before 1545, and was owned in King Charles
the First's time by one Collins who entertained Fairfax as his
guest. Here in the dining-room, Cromwell made Fairfax comman-
der of the armies of the west, and here the Treaty of the West was
signed.

In 1796 Colonel James Coleridge, S.T.Coleridge's eldest and
stuffiest brother, had bought the Chanter's House; it had been the
home of the three Coleridge judges: James's son John Taylor
Coleridge, his son John Duke Coleridge (the Lord Chief Justice
and first Baron Coleridge), and his son Bernard, father of Geoffrey
the Lord Coleridge of the day. The garden entrance was the original
one, the rooms on either side and above belonging to the old house:
the remainder was nineteenth-century. The dining-room, now a
chief glory, is the old room as it was, except for the enlargement of
the south windows and for the beautiful panelling in elm off the
estate.

My first impression was of family portraits dominating the
dining-room, parlour, hall, and library, portraits of the three
judges and many others. Through the library I was led to a small
conservatory in the middle of which was a tall myrtle bush. Could

it be the one on Coleridge's bedside table that had burst into bloom at his death? 'The very one. Fancy you knowing that!' Lady Coleridge told how on his death it had been taken to Ottery for safety in the warm Devon climate, but in 'The Great Frost' of 1929 they 'though it was a goner' and moved it into the conservatory where it flourishes and blooms riotously every year.

Lady Coleridge was quick at making connexions; we at once discovered the drops of Irish in each other, 'the leaven in the English lump,' she said. When she asked directly what my interest in the Chanter's House was, I could see even her self-control quail when I said it was chiefly in any manuscripts and annotated books of the poet in the library. Not a word was said, and I was shown the S.T.Coleridge alcove. The first moment of seeing the man's own books, notebooks, and handwriting, was like taking a breath of air from some other climate of existence. (Was Coleridge right in thinking the tangible the lesser reality?) Established at a big comfortable desk in front of the shelves of his books and manuscripts, what was I to do? Sit and browse? I was stunned not only by the sensory experience but by the quantity before me.

At lunch she explained to Lord Coleridge that it was not after all an old house and old furniture that I was come to see—had Mrs Boyle suggested that?—but the library. There was a moment of silence clearly labelled 'No comment' and then some bantering from 'Himself', as Lady Coleridge referred to him, avoiding the title and first names. The banter mounted in him as it brought out the Irish in me. Geoffrey Coleridge had a brusque, dry, caustic tongue which could be rude or frightening if intuition didn't tell one that the last thing to do was be offended or frightened. With Lady Coleridge's gentle encouragement I cheerfully returned his grapeshot.

He continued: 'Old Sam was only a poet, you know, never did anything practical that was any good to anybody, actually not thought much of in the family, a bit of a disgrace in fact, taking drugs and not looking after his wife and children. Of course STC must have been a *wonderful man*—in a way—he was somehow clever enough to take in so many great men—but why a young girl like you should spend your time on the old reprobate, I can't think! All those badly-written scribblings—couldn't even write a decent hand that ordinary people can read—full of stuff and nonsense. But all you pedants *live* on this sort of thing. Useless knowledge, perfectly useless. Now I at least know something about beef cattle . . .

'What kind of cattle?' I asked, and blessed an uncle who had kept Holsteins and talked a good deal about them. So there followed a conversation about cattle before we got back to STC.

'You know I'm not a *direct* descendant of that fellow, don't you? Ours is the legal side—much better.'

There followed, in response to my questions about the portraits round the room, a description of Sir John Taylor Coleridge, Member of Parliament for Exeter, a Judge of the Queen's Bench and a Privy Councillor, a kindly figure regarded as almost saintly in the family; there were many drawings of his beautiful face in the house. He was proud of 'Uncle Sam' and used to take his friends to meet him in Highgate. His son, John Duke, who became Lord Chief Justice, had the largest portrait; it presided over the whole room. Much was left unsaid about him, I felt. But his son, Bernard Lord Coleridge, Geoffrey's father, was spoken of with warm affection.

'Yes—wonderful man, my father, with such *knowledge*! He would have been able to talk with you about the poet, and put you in your place, too, you little bookworm! He knew books, and he knew the world, the most just and kindest of men. You should have known my father. I don't suppose you've read *his* books—much better than STC's, but you've got your nose too much in him to bother with good solid human books.' In later years he presented me with those books, and I came to recognize that whenever he said, as he did several times, 'How I wish you had known my father!' he was paying me his highest most affectionate compliment. But for now the banter went on.

'What do you suppose *he* looked like, your old poet? Every portrait looks different from every other. No two the same fellow, don't you think?'

'"Coleridge of the godlike forehead",' I quoted. 'Big grey eyes under that prominent brow—an open face—a bit more cherubic than any I see in this room—a tallish man—taller than you!' He took that with a twinkle.

'Now, now—that old man in the drawing we have at the fireplace in the front parlour there looks absolutely the miserable invalid. Old, I suppose?'

Northcote's portrait, of a younger STC, was all eyes, very animated, I pointed out, with a mop of unruly hair, a plumpish face
and almost too sweet an expression. Allston's was very dignified;
Coleridge the public lecturer, head erect, a quiet, commanding
talker, relaxed. They all suggest a soft tender skin.

'But how on earth can a painter catch genius, so mercurial a
genius? Hazlitt said Coleridge was the only man he ever met who
answered to his idea of genius. But I don't think about Coleridge's
physical appearance very much at all. I just have the sense of a
gentle but animated, inquiring, kindly companionable person,
doing more than his share of the talk.'

'Didn't Wordsworth say he was the most wonderful man he had
ever known? I can't believe it.'

So I told them about the old sexton of Highgate Church, after
STC's death, describing him to a visitor as walking more than an
hour at a time under the great trees in the Grove, with his hat off
and a book in his hand.

'That is how I see Coleridge.'

'And with children about him,' Lady Coleridge added. She
thought she had seen an engraving rather like that.

In that beautiful dining-room I noticed a plaque commemorating
the occasion of a presentation to Fairfax as leader of the Parlia-
mentarian forces in the Civil War, in 1642.

'Yes, always a bit red, the Devonshire people,' Lord Coleridge
growled. 'Leftish, even then, Devon folk. But that centre-piece
there, I don't suppose with your head in the STC clouds you'd
know anything about that?'

It was a large silver cup, of which the black mount bore an en-
graved silver plate recording that the cup was presented to Governor
Simcoe by the House of Upper Canada on the occasion of his
retirement as Governor of Upper Canada in 1796. (1796 was a year
more important in my mind for another event: Coleridge's first
volume of poems.) In the ensuing dialogue it became apparent that
I knew more about the life in Canada of the Simcoes, once the
Devon neighbours of the Coleridges, then Geoffrey did, which
somehow pleased him, so that we easily got on to genial, sympathetic terms. He had not heard of *Mrs Simcoe's Diary*, an old
favourite of mine, and like many English people he loved hearing
about early pioneer experiences, and anything to do with Indians.

I think he recognized that I had interests in addition to 'the old poet'.

In one argumentative round I won a modest victory. I felt, especially on this first acquaintance, somehow in a constant sparring match with him. I had referred to 'the Canadian fall'.

'It may be "the fall" in Canada,' he said, 'I know you Yanks use these awful expressions, but in England we say "the autumn".' (He also liked to tease Canadians by lumping us together with the 'Yanks'.) And so I read aloud from the inscribed tablet on the wall, which I had examined just that morning.

'In this Convention Room Oliver Cromwell *in the fall of the year 1645* convened the people of the town and neighbourhood and demanded of them men and money for the Civil War. Here also on October 29th Members of Parliament on behalf of both Houses presented Sir Thomas Fairfax with a fair Jewel and hung it about his neck in honour of his skill and valour at Naseby Fight.'

Turning a slight discomfiture into the companionableness that was the more attractive side of him, he said, 'Well, "fall o' the leaf" —I suppose in its origin it *is* a charming expression. From now on I shall have to think of it that way. You win, Bookie. And I'm going to call you Bookie from now on, for a bookworm is obviously what you are.'

I was asked back for luncheon and to visit the library on each of the three remaining days of my stay in Sidmouth, but it was difficult to decide how best to use the time. Confronted by fifty-five notebooks, two hundred books, many annotated, and the files of family letters, what could one do? Certainly not sit and croon over the maligned handwriting—the sharp emotions of first handling the notebooks had to be quickly absorbed. I decided to make a list, as descriptive and accurate as possible, of everything there, fearing I might never see those manuscripts and books again.

The long library, built by Butterfield for the Lord Chief Justice as a new wing, had a fireplace at each end, and a gallery on the east. The whole west side between the great windows was given over to law books; and on the east were four alcoves full of various sorts of books and another fireplace. Beside this last, the favourite cosy corner at tea-time and in the evenings, stood Lady Coleridge's sewing basket and little tables for her husband's pipes and periodicals.

One alcove was wholly devoted to STC and family books and papers. STC's notebooks, covering his whole adult life, filled a top shelf; down below were various other manuscripts, in his own hand or transcribed by members of the family or others. His annotated books filled several shelves, except that his neat collected set of the Waverley novels (Scott presumably being deemed 'human books') was among the run-of-the-mill volumes elsewhere. There were also family letter-books, editions of STC's works by his children, Sara and Derwent, and Henry Nelson Coleridge (HNC) his nephew who married Sara, the usual books about STC, books by other Colcridges like Stephen the anti-vivisectionist, and the memoirs of the judges. There were a few volumes of poems by other Coleridges also: by Ernest Hartley Coleridge (EHC), the grandson who did the first Oxford edition of the poems and who made a charming selection from the notebooks entitled *Anima Poetae*; one or two volumes by 'old Gilbert', son of the Lord Chief Justice, still alive and a magistrate, somewhere in his seventies; and of the later offspring the one that had drunk more of the milk of paradise than most, Mary Elizabeth Coleridge, STC's great great niece. Beside Mary's volumes were almost all the works of her close friend, Charlotte M. Yonge. There were odd out-of-the-way things such as survive only in the family: a printed memoir of Sara (Mrs HNC) by her daughter, Edith, the only copy I have ever seen; a few copies of HNC's *Six Months in the West in 1825* (the rest of the first edition having been destroyed by parental command because of a 'disrespectful' reference in the early pages to Aunt Elizabeth's medicine chest as 'The Cave of Death'); a commentary on the *Book of Judges* by the old Reverend John, the vicar and Ottery schoolmaster (STC's father), as obscure and learned as his Hebrew-besprinkled sermons, though those were beloved of his parishioners because in them the Scriptures were given to them in 'the very language of the Holy Ghost,' they said.

The temptations to stray into the Coleridge labyrinth were legion, and powerful, but with a few lapses I did persevere with my list, an instinctive procedure not clearly directed towards any

specific plan, but crucially useful twenty years on. At this early
time it seemed simply that a list of annotated books would be a
clue to STC's reading, and a descriptive account of the notebooks
could give their dates, watermarks, and a survey, however rough,
of their main contents. It took the three remaining days working
at full speed to do this, and on the last afternoon the electric power
suddenly went off at about three o'clock—in late December that
meant near-darkness. There ensued a great rushing about by
'Himself', servants, everyone, in search of candelabra to set up
around me for light—sixteen candle-power in the end. No one
could have been more hospitable, a fact even more appreciated
when I learned later that he had not wanted me there at all and did
not ordinarily permit scholars to use the library. Once admitted I
had only a very courteous welcome. When I asked to be allowed
again in the first Easter vacation, however, I was refused, on the
ground that if I were admitted he could not shut the door to other
students.

London and the British Museum occupied the rest of the first
vacation—a mixed feast of manuscripts and theatre. From the BM
catalogue I ordered all the philosophical books annotated by
Coleridge, and most important, in the light of my recent post-
graduate work in Toronto, Tennemann's *Geschichte der Philosophie*.
Coleridge had possessed ten of the eleven volumes, and his annotations were as exciting as Tennemann was dull. Coleridge ran the
gamut of the history of western philosophy from the pre-Socratics
to the post-Kantians, attacking Tennemann for a narrow Kantianism, for bad German, for complacency, and for lack of imagination
as to the ancients; in short, here was Coleridge in the thick of
battle, at close grips with an author, sometimes pursuing the foot-
notes to their sources, using his powers of generalization and cross-
relation in the vast vista, and at the same time making minute
incisive penetrations, in short, working at once as a poet and as a
logician. I copied out every annotation, with the German passage
from which it took off in a second colour of ink, and bore down on
Miss Seaton at the beginning of the next term. She agreed that the
editing of these would give me another opportunity to search out
Coleridge, and could constitute, with a suitable introduction and
notes, a B. Litt. thesis.

It was clear to me, struggling with Tennemann's page-long

sentences, that I should need to spend the summer in Germany improving on my school German. Another lucky conversation, over coffee in someone's room, led to an introduction to Herr Max and Frau Irma von Ruperti and their four children, and a summer in Allenstein, in East Prussia. The *au pair* plan was that my share was the travel expense of the journey and speaking English half a day, theirs my room and board and German the other half-day. The summer was an unforgettable one, as the first journey abroad to a country of another language and because of the family itself. Herr von Ruperti as the *Regierungs-Präsident*, a sort of Lieutenant-Governor, of south-east Prussia, lived in the ancient castle, from the tower of which, it was thought, Copernicus had made some of his observations—some of the diagrams on the walls of the tower were said to be his. Though in 1931 the family, still feeling the financial losses of World War I and the post-war inflation, was living frugally in private, they occasionally had important visitors to entertain more lavishly. General von Mackensen, the victor of Tannenberg, a lively gentleman of eighty-five without cane or spectacles, came with his son and daughter-in-law to dinner. The latter provided me (this was August 1931) with my first experience of a Nazi; she was one of the most politically aggressive women I have ever encountered. In her undergraduate days at the University of Königsberg she had been president of a student organization which obtained the dismissal of the head of the university. I understood he had refused the distribution of a Nazi pamphlet, or forbidden the use of a university hall for a Hitlerite political meeting, or some such thing. It was a rude awakening for me. I was fairly well accustomed in my own argumentative family to political and social discussions of a contentious sort, but all that was mere argument, words, in a calm Canadian backwater; here international tensions were felt on the skin. I remember the shock of hearing the quite a-political Frau von Ruperti burst forth against Edward VII ('the Peacemaker!') as the real culprit in starting World War I, the Triple Entente, &c. I saw in fact how reduced by the inflation were people of wealth, like the Rupertis—millionaires before the war and now allowing but one white roll for breakfast. Also how the emphasis in the schools was on building children physically strong—'English sports'—politically informed, and nationally sorry for themselves. It was all rather alarming and

conflict-making to an innocent abroad. One felt the individual
Germans so civilized, yet often ingenuous, sometimes disingenuous too, suffering, and victimized by their highly-centralized
Bismarckian system, yet also full of anti-Semitic, anti-French, anti-
English anger, providing justifications that could not be swept
under the mat for the belligerent anti-German charges being
levelled by Churchill in the early thirties. What I saw and heard
helped not only to light dynamite under any casual Canadian
assumptions; the experiences later also put flesh on some of
Coleridge's views about society, morals, and politics.

When I was about to leave Allenstein in September 1931, England
suddenly went off the gold standard. There was much complacent
nodding of heads. France was to blame. Now England would learn
what France was, would know that France, not Germany, was
really the enemy, etc, etc, how are the mighty fallen! Yet by the
next day a soberer tone prevailed. England was after all less an
enemy than France—better to have a strong friend than a weak
one—and what would happen to the world at large if sterling
became shaky? For me there was a very direct personal realization
of what it meant. My English money was at once worth half of
what it had been. The sum that was to have taken me back across
Germany, a fortnight's zig-zag trip, was the student's usual no-
more-than-enough. Herr von Ruperti insisted on lending me some
cash, but when I got as far as Cologne I had in my purse a twenty-
five-dollar Canadian Pacific Express money order from father, and
not much else. I had thought to fly from Cologne to London,
saving the extra two or three days' expenses, but alas, the last
flight of the season had left a few hours before I arrived. It was a
week-end and no banks open. A Swiss hotel-keeper took me in, very
vague about the validity and value of my twenty-five-dollar Canadian Pacific Express order, but finally he advanced me less than it
was worth, promising to refund to Oxford any surplus, a promise
honestly carried out. The return journey across Germany was thus
a trying experience, from which, however, with the Ruperti training behind me, I learned more German in the two weeks than in the
previous sheltered two months. And there were splendid moments—
like a performance of *Die Meistersinger* in Königsberg, of *Salome* in
Berlin. Darker moments too, with a sinister 'guide' in Heidelberg,
and a hungry young woman student, acting as guide in Berlin who

ordered, for the tea which I could ill afford but to which I had invited her, all the most expensive things on the menu, not realizing that I was a student too and had nothing to spare, though I doubt if she would have cared if she had; she was hard and hungry, and exploiting a former enemy.

In the end there was the lovely moment of landing back in England, and the train at Dover. It was a homecoming—all those amusing old porters on the pier, so fatherly and friendly compared with the European ones. I bought *The Times* and sank back into the railway carriage, glad to *have been* abroad, very happy to be 'home', a feeling everyone who has had any luck at all in life must know.

The return to Oxford is much richer than the first arrival. For me it was a return to freedom—I was free from examinations to work all out on the thesis. It was a return, not to College with its noisy hordes and the eleven o'clock curfew, but to the seclusion of digs, a bed-sitter in St John's Road in the house of crisp Mrs Jessop, who was an excellent cook and loved to feast my friends. Especially 'Mr Wallace' of whom as an ice hockey player she was an idolatrous fan. It was a return to almost daily skating with him on the ice-rink. One night that winter William almost by accident won the British Indoor Skating Championship for the mile, hard upon taking some girl out to a big dinner, and suddenly rushing off to the arena, changing into tights and his skates in the taxi, and leaping on to the ice as the gong went. He returned to Oxford with a monstrous silver cup out of which we all drank champagne while we made him parade in the borrowed tights, three sizes too large for him, in which he had won the race. He and his New College friends also corrected the Greek in my thesis, putting me in my place in all sorts of ways. The Scout used to appear at midnight, regularly apologizing for the fact that the rules required him to evict me, but knowing full well that my bicycle stood outside immediately under the Common Room window of Savile House and that once he and I had both observed the rule, I would be helped back in again over the sill. The boys could not accompany me to my digs for they were all still under curfew. I taught some of them to paddle a canoe, which helped to balance their superiority in so many other respects.

The fourth Oxford term was perhaps above all a return to the river and canoeing, particularly with 'Thorney'.

If Miss Seaton was St Hugh's first gift to me, Gertrude Thorneycroft was another. She was the college bursar, and the only English person I found in Oxford who knew how to handle a paddle. She had been instrumental in the purchase of a good Peterborough cedar-strip canoe by the Senior Common Room. The paddles however being execrable, I quickly sent home for some decent ones, and we spent many a Sunday on the Cherwell, the Thames, the Evenlode and the Windrush, sometimes taking the canoe round to Port Meadow the Saturday night before to get a good start next morning. Not only were the exercise and the quiet rhythm of the canoe in Thorney's firm and gentle company good for body and soul, but the short trips led to longer ones—for instance, to Stratford-on-Avon via the Leamington Canal, and through the Warwick estate (by permission); and down the Severn through the pottery towns and by train portage to Cricklade, the head of the Thames, and so back to Oxford. On these longer trips I saw England by the back door, and became the more conscious of some realities not evident in Oxford.

There were other expeditions with her, musical ones, to Covent Garden by car—the whole cycle of *The Ring* with Flagstad, Melchior and Lotte Lehmann, driving back on the great northwest road after midnight with the car lights glaring into hundreds of rabbits' eyes; in Oxford Thorney introduced me to the Beethoven Quartets, all of them, played by the Lener Quartet of Budapest, perhaps the greatest musical experience of a lifetime. There were walking trips, Sundays in the Chilterns or the Cotswolds, and longer ones to the glorious northwest coast of Devon whence the Ancient Mariner when he was a young man about Coleridge's age set sail. On the Quantocks we too 'wandered in gladness' and saw too,

'On springy heath, along the hill-top edge,
The roaring dell o'erwooded, narrow, deep,'
in which certain
'. . . few poor yellow leaves
Ne'er tremble in the gale, yet tremble still,
Fanned by the waterfall!'
How all these delights contributed precisely to Coleridge studies it defeats me to say, but I know it would be graceless to forget what a rich atmosphere of helpfulness and affection those Oxford dons

created for me. (Of course we poked fun at them, criticized them, disliked some of them. But *Gaudy Night* be damned. Dorothy Sayers told at most a very small part of the truth, in my experience.) Nor was I alone in receiving these attentions. The Seaton and the Thorney frequently took students to plays and concerts, Thorney especially was noted for knowledge of and kindness to students, new and old; never fully identified with Oxford, she had a particularly soft spot for those students farthest away from home.

True, St Hugh's at that time was not intellectually very exciting, from my angle at least, but if I seem to be romanticizing about its other virtues, I would point out that I had no doubt a certain advantage in being a post-graduate student a year or two more mature than most, and a Canadian, and therefore free of all sorts of ties (old school and other) and associations. I had already taken one post-graduate degree and had done a little university teaching and supervising, which put me somewhere between student and don. In a day when accents were still oppressively significant of social status in Oxford, it was comfortable to be a Canadian to whom the snobbish norms were not applicable. Perhaps, I sometimes thought, it was helpful too to have had a fairly uninhibited upbringing in the parsonage, in particular in a family that paid no attention whatever to social class.

I was aware that to some of my compatriots Oxford was often distasteful, snobbish, provincial, decadent, even cruel; I saw these negatives too, but I could see no reason why I should not enjoy all its great positive glories while I was among them. That was what I was there for. So I answered the sensitive consciences of the dissidents with something about the unwisdom, at least in some circumstances, of kicking against the pricks.

Oxford set me to work with zest, and taught me the virtue of not working all the time.

In the second year, as I worked on Coleridge's marginal notes on Tennemann (Frau von Ruperti had found a second-hand copy of the right edition for me in Königsberg), one question became increasingly puzzling. Why did Coleridge go on reading this tiresome, windy *History of Philosophy* in very dull German when he was in such constant disagreement with the author, so impatient and irritated with Tennemann's 'cowed' and 'misunderstood Kantianism', distorting the critical insights of 'the great Master'? He must

have been reading for some practical purpose of his own. What?
Did Tennemann provide him with the chronological outline and
other material information for his course of lectures on the
History of Philosophy in 1818–19? In a footnote in the *Letters of
Samuel Taylor Coleridge*, Ernest Hartley Coleridge, his grandson,
had written, after quoting the 'Prospectus', 'A reporter was hired
at the expense of Hookham Frere to take down the lectures in
shorthand. A transcript, which I possess, contains numerous errors
and omissions, but it is interesting as affording proof of the conversational style of Coleridge's lectures . . .' and he referred the
reader to J.Dykes Campbell's biography. Where then were these
lecture reports? They would surely provide the clue as to the use
made of 'old Tinny man', as Coleridge called him.

I wrote to Ernest Hartley Coleridge's son, the Rev. G.H.B.
Coleridge in Leatherhead, to inquire, or possibly it was a less
specific letter asking if I could see him; however it was, my first
visit to Leatherhead was made startling in the first instant by the
boy who answered the door. His face brought Hartley to life.

I remember quite a good serious talk over tea with Mr and Mrs
Coleridge about STC, with again some of the half-jest half-earnest
chaffing of Ottery, but in a rather different key. In the study there
were more annotated books, a few notebooks, and many binders
full of transcriptions in various hands, predominantly the hand of
GHB's father, Ernest Hartley Coleridge. But no, Mr Coleridge
said, he did not know where the philosophical lecture reports had
gone. He knew they had existed, the shorthand transcribed in
long-hand, and he reached for his copy of his father's edition of the
Letters and pointed to the footnote. He opined, as the date of this
the last reference to them was 1895, that perhaps the lecture
reports had been in a trunk full of biographical materials lost in
1895 somewhere between London and Torquay. It had been a
great grief to his father, and disheartened him about going on with
his proposed life of the poet. No, no other member of the family
would have them, or know any more about them. No, they were
not at Ottery, and he told how his father, conducting his private
schools and losing money on one after another (perhaps a touch of
STC's father, the schoolmaster-vicar about him?), finally had had
to decide, in order to finance a Cambridge education for him, to
sell fifty-five notebooks and other manuscripts and nearly two

hundred of STC's books, to his cousin Lord Chief Justice Coleridge; but he was sure he philosophical lecture reports were not among them.

Here was a dead end. Wild thoughts arose in my mind, with all the impetuosity and tenacity of the post-graduate student, of making a journey from Paddington to Torquay, getting off at every station en route and searching the left-luggage rooms all along the line. In England could one not easily imagine a box resting dustily in some dark corner for thirty-five years? But it was pointed out by sceptical discouragers that between 1895 and 1931 there had been a World War, also many unknown changes in railway routes. Besides, even had I been more than half-serious, I could not have found enough time for such an admittedly hare-brained expedition. So, in the thesis I merely speculated on the problem, making out as strong a case as I could, in the teeth of some of the doubting Thomases that always surround Coleridge, that the course of lectures had actually been delivered to the public, and that for those who disbelieved in the actuality of the reports (some argued that they must be of other lectures, literary ones) there was a certain amount of evidence to be collected from Coleridge's reading and letters of that period, and from newspaper accounts. The relation to Tennemann, however, remained unproven.

That was summer 1932, and I had to return to Canada. Though for degree purposes the thesis was completed and accepted, I had a sense of something unfinished. The wrench of leaving the bliss and blessings of Oxford, English friends, and an England which I had come to love and admire, was the severest parting I had ever experienced. Could I ever finance a return? Could the philosophical lectures mystery ever be solved? Somehow I felt there was an answer.

II

1933–1936

It is sometimes useful in scholarly work to be tantalized.

When I returned from England in 1932, my benign Victoria College found me a job. Depression conditions were severe in Canada. A series of wheat-harvest failures—five, I believe—added to the world-wide stock-market crash, meant unprecedented unemployment and, in this land of plenty, hunger. It was a godsend to be asked to be assistant to an interim Dean of Women, Norma Ford, and to spend a third of my time teaching in the English department. This meant living in the undergraduate residence, Annesley Hall, as a don, administering rules I did not believe in, and lecturing three times a week to the first-year students not specializing in English in the General Course. It meant reading hundreds of essays, and fifteen hundred dollars a year.

Coleridge was right in advising young men desiring to become authors not to make authorship a full-time occupation. To quote that eleventh chapter of *Biographia Literaria*, which Herbert Read said he took much to heart, 'never pursue literature as a trade. With one exception of one extraordinary man, I have never known an individual of genius, healthy or happy without a profession, i.e. some regular employment, which does not depend on the will of the moment...' 'Regular employment' left little time in the early years for that 'will of the moment'. Yet the lost lecture reports never were far from my mind. Correspondence with various other members of the Coleridge family, some quite distantly related, produced no new information. But were those lecture reports really lost? They had once been seen. They were not a fantasy. They must have constituted a fairly bulky manuscript. Unless someone destroyed them they must surely be somewhere.

In the summer of 1933 I was once more back in London. This was before the days when flying became routine, and long before the days of student rates. I travelled by sea, third class, after a

couple of years of scrimping and saving on a bottom-of-the-ladder
salary, and the sense of achievement merely in getting there was an
exciting part of the pleasure that propelled one. Why did I go?
Because I had been. And to this day I never arrive in London
without joy and never leave without regret. 'The country habit has
me by the heart,' Vita Sackville-West said. Me, too; and so has the
London habit.

The next Coleridge steps were not clear, but might be clarified
by another session with the manuscripts in the British Museum,
rich quarries still unmined.

However, the long searches through the memoirs of persons
who might have attended the lectures yielded no clues to the fate
of the lecture reports. Manuscript fragments of Coleridge were
more rewarding, but only in other respects; they did sharpen my
increasing amazement at the modernity of his thought—his interest
in 'animal magnetism' or mesmerism, a form of hypnosis, and its
psychological implications; his thoughts about language and human
communication, about the education of children, about logic as by
no means limited to Aristotle, about the animal, vegetable, and
mineral worlds and their margins and, perhaps above all, his sensitive observations of both natural and human phenomena. I was
getting in deeper and deeper.

I also had more questions for the Reverend G.H.B.Coleridge at
Leatherhead, who was as genial and approachable by Coleridgians
as his cousin Geoffrey Lord Coleridge was not. So I found myself
invited to lunch with the Vicar and Mrs Coleridge, and asking if
there had been any further leads at all as to the whereabouts of the
reports of the Philosophical Lectures. The answer was what I had
anticipated. But was there nothing else I was interested in? So I
said I should like, if it were permissible, to make a list of the
annotated books and the manuscripts in his collection, as I had
done at Ottery; not to be nosey, just to get some approximate
overall view.

'Why a young girl like you wants to spend a beautiful sunny
afternoon like this among fusty old books mystifies me,' Mr
Coleridge said, 'but if that's your way of enjoying yourself . . .'

'For many a summer I have been and shall be drinking in the sun
and wind on the most beautiful fresh waters in the world,' I said,
'on canoe trips through lakes and rivers where my companion and

I for a week at a time have seen not a soul, and read only the one book we allowed ourselves in our packs. Is it so bad to live in a library for an afternoon?' After a question or two about bears and Indians in our northern bush, he unlocked his cupboard. I was turned loose in the library.

'Look into those shelves there, and these cupboards here,' he said. 'Make yourself at home. I have to go to a parish meeting, but I'll be back for tea.'

In making my list I came to one cupboard different from the rest, a very deep one. It looked as if it had been an old chimney at some time, but now it was lined and shelved. I began with the great folio volumes on the lower shelves, and when I had worked up to a shelf just above waist height, the cupboard seemed to become deeper; it was necessary, in order to see things at the back, practically to swim breast-stroke into the cupboard. In this awkward horizontal stretch I saw, in the dim recesses, positively leaping out of the darkness, a pile of folio-size booklets in soft marbled-paper covers. They could be only one thing. Reports of twelve of the fourteen lectures of the Philosophical course, verbatim and neatly in order! Backing off the shelf with the loot, I saw that No. 1 was missing, and No. 14, but substantially the course was there, each lecture dated. With the swoop of a sea-gull, or something less graceful plunging for a meal, I dived into Lecture 3, and from the first few pages came up with my fish—a specific reference to Tennemann.

The Reverend Gerard Coleridge came home from his parish meeting to find a gibbering idiot in his study. He seemed as pleased as I was, and as non-plussed as to what to do next. Even the brief glances at the manuscript told me I longed to edit it—a Chinese-puzzle of a manuscript, in the impersonal clerkly hand of the reporter, almost totally without punctuation of any kind, with blanks where the names of most of the philosophers should have been and wherever there was a Latin or Greek quotation. The reporter evidently knew no philosophy and no philosophers, nor was he up to even the smallest classical tags; and there were other gaps when perhaps Coleridge mumbled, or latecomers were noisy and the reporter could not hear. Many guessing games would have to be played. A note by Ernest Hartley Coleridge attached to the manuscript said, 'Coleridge's notes for these lectures are in Notebook 25.' No other lectures of Coleridge had been taken down in shorthand by a professional reporter, and of no other of his seven lecture courses was there so complete a record.

That night in the Bull in Leatherhead, for the first time in my life I ordered a beautiful claret with a solitary dinner.

But there was a catch. Notebook 25 would be essential for the editing. It was in my Ottery list, and no scholars were allowed there. After all, the library was their living-room, where 'Himself' read his paper and 'Herself' did her mending. My working there meant an invasion. However, I wanted in any case to read these lecture reports and begged Mr Coleridge to allow me to send them to the Bodleian Library, on loan. There I could consult the Oxford people and perhaps do something useful with them. A timely fib from a sub-librarian saved those reports from being sent straight back to Mr Coleridge—for I had not gone through the necessary formalities of arranging the holding of a borrowed manuscript with the Librarian. It was another undeserved piece of good fortune for me that Owen Holloway was willing to perjure his soul for the sake of what he had the grace to believe was scholarship.

Miss Seaton at once came to Bodley, much excited. I must edit these reports, the manuscript of which we should refer to as 'X' in public places; places like the ladies washroom of the BM, I remember, or even college corridors! It seemed an unnecessary compounding of mystery, but all part of the fun. She also said I should ask the Principal to write to Lord Coleridge to tell him I must see Notebook 25. I knew we should not say must!

The Principal with her usual zest entered into the campaign, but felt that I should write to him myself. She put the case very clearly.

'After all, when you asked before, you had no specific problem to solve.' I objected that a brash 'colonial' intruder was the last thing I wanted to be. Whereupon I received a memorable and invaluable lecture. In the first place, Lord Coleridge could only say no, and what harm in receiving a negative? In the second place, I must become aware that scholarship is bigger than the person involved in it, and therefore requests made in the name of learning cease to be merely personal requests. This one had little to do with me, and that little only incidentally. I was merely the vehicle, trying to present an unpublished work to the world.

So, with some misgivings, and also the queer feeling of an

unbelievable state of affairs, when something so desired by me personally should also represent, to a high-minded observer, something significant for the learned world, I wrote (and several times re-drafted) a letter, explaining my problem. As a result of finding the Philosophical Lectures, I needed to see Notebook 25, and Coleridge's notes for them, and that without them the work could not be properly edited. Back came a postcard from Lady Coleridge —from Arisaig, Scotland, bearing the date of their return home and an invitation. Would I not spend a fortnight with them? 'We are close by here motoring about Scotland, shan't be home for another fortnight.'

The first of many visits as a house-guest, in July 1933, could not not have been more charming. I was put in the Great Parlour Chamber, at the front of the old part of the house, overlooking the goldfish pond on the lawn, the yews and the ilexes, and with a glimpse of the church tower through an east window. The four-poster faced deep-set windows in walls two feet thick, hung with coarse dark red linen on large old wooden curtain rods. Furniture of every sort of English period, a French-looking safe, a commode, a washstand with its full complement of crockery, hot-water cans, all; a tall rosewood tallboy with a model of a Chinese junk sitting on it; a huge high sofa, three or four stuffed chairs, a large chest of drawers, wardrobe, a large bookcase, some small chairs and tables, a dressing table with a bowl of roses and a bouquet of Sweet William, all sorts of knick-knacks—an enchanting room full of little comforts, and every attention down to the biscuit jar on the night table. It was also a room full of engravings of S.T.Coleridge and other members of the family. For years to come, I was made to think of it as my room. After tea and talk I took to the library.

Notebook 25 was nowhere to be found. Lord Coleridge did not seem perturbed, but that notebook was not with the others. True, some were and long had been missing from the series; 29, 31, and 32, for instance. But I had seen Notebook 25 in 1930, had it on my list, had made notes about it in that very library.

In the Coleridge alcove I lifted every book and every manuscript off the shelves, but it was not there; there was a slight gap on the shelf where it had been. So I began a systematic search of the whole library, section by section, shelf by shelf, beginning at the south end, to the left of the entrance, working my way then along the west side, then the north, through history, travel, and long unlikely-looking rows of totally irrelevant law books. On the last afternoon of my visit, in the only as yet unsearched section of the library, immediately to the *right* of the entrance, Notebook 25 turned up among some French novels and, in a light brownish cover, looking very like them. The explanation, delved out and deduced by bits and pieces later, was that on receiving my plea to see Notebook 25, Geoffrey Coleridge had taken it down from its place on the high shelf to see if the notes for the Philosophical Lectures were in fact there. Finding my request valid, he permitted the invitation. But having looked at Notebook 25, and being interrupted by the announcement of a visitor, or luncheon, as he left the library he put it down on the shelf nearest the door. The parlourmaid, or someone tidying up, then rammed it in among the brown paper-bound books just above the ledge on which it lay.

I saw that there were at least one hundred and twenty-three pages of notes closely written in it for the Philosophical Lectures. Thoughts of spending the night frantically copying naturally occurred to me, of asking to be excused from dining, perhaps taking a later train on the morrow. But there were guests to dinner—and anyhow, it looked hopelessly impossible to get through it, to be accurate, to read all the pinched Greek and later insertions and corrections in the inner margins. What to do? I had a date to pick black currants with Lady Coleridge in the garden. As we picked, I told her my plight. It was her habit to set her mind to work at once on a problem; of many endearing characteristics, one that was unfailing was her resourcefulness for anyone in any sort of disaster.

'Don't worry, Bookie, but of course you may not be excused from dinner, you may *not* sit up all night. And you *must* go tomorrow because we're to be quarantined with Cousin V—coming here for the purpose. Lord Coleridge will *lend* you the notebook, I'm sure . . . Ask him.' Then after some protest from me and further talk about the notebook, she said, 'You know, Bookie, I always find a good time to broach these things is just after dinner— after he has had his port!' Loyalty to him was betrayed not a jot, but she was on my side. Later, then, on the terrace, under 'that green light that lingers in the West', a heavenly summer night, the following conversation took place. Seeing at a glance that I was incapable of opening the subject, she did it herself.

'Geoff, do you know what's happened to this poor child?'

'Mercy, what?'

'Tell him, Bookie!'

So I stammered out the business about finding Notebook 25 among the paperback French novels; I still couldn't bring myself to utter the language of borrowing and lending.

'You could lend her the notebook, couldn't you, Geoff?' she said. He turned quickly to me, but with a twinkle in his eye, as much as to say, 'You've been getting round my wife!' What he actually said was,

'Nonsense! Why can't she stay on another fortnight and scribble away to her heart's content?'

'Because Cousin V is coming down here to-morrow to be in quarantine, and this poor little creature would not be allowed to escape for the duration. She has to get back to her students.'

'A pity, but of course it would save us from having the bother of having her about the place. What will you do with it if I lend it to you, Bookie?'

That problem had been occupying my mind all the afternoon.

'Put it in my bank in London for safekeeping,' I said, 'and then ask the Royal Photographic Society whom they would recommend for such work, and have the relevant pages photographed.'

'It wouldn't damage the notebook?'

'If it would, I wouldn't have it done.'

'It's a family heirloom you know, Bookie . . .'

Lady Coleridge: 'Oh, Geoff! She'll be far more careful of it than you ever would be and you know it!' He had no ready reply to that; he probably was well aware he had mislaid it.

'How would you get it back here?'

Lady Coleridge: 'Tim's coming you know, in September.'

Geoff: 'Tim would be frightened to death to have it on her person!'

'Of course I should be more than willing to bring it myself,' I said.

'And eat more of our grapes? Nothing doing, Bookie. Tim will bring it. Serves her right! She'll be frightened to death to carry it! But it serves her right for landing you on us. She says you're all right—so I suppose you are. But look here—have you shut up the chickens tonight, you two conspirators? What good are you? I'm going to take the dog for a run. Poor old girl hasn't been out much to-day . . .'

So that was it! I had not known that Aunt Tim—Miss Katherine Alethea Marguerite Mackarness in Oxford, Daisy to her friends, Tim to the Coleridges for her timidity—had been the instrument through whom Mrs Boyle had found the way to Ottery for me in the first place, and she would now do penance by bearing the notebook back there. Lord and Lady Coleridge were fond of her; owing to their family marriages she was aunt to both of them. She had looked me up at St Hugh's after my first trip to Ottery, invited me often to 32 Leckford Road to tea, and I her to college, sometimes in the garden, sometimes in my room. She was a dear gentle Dresden china creature with a very strong mind of her own. She was the oil on all the troubled family waters, almost the only Coleridge I ever met who was known and truly beloved by the Ottery cousins and the poet's direct descendants. She had told them I was a lady and would not walk off with their manuscripts, and that I really was working on Coleridge, and that she felt warmly towards me. This was the reason for the fortnight's invitation, and for the loan of the notebook. To this day I have not discovered whether Mrs Boyle was guileless and just a trifle vague about introducing me through Miss Mackarness as interested in old houses; quite possibly she knew very well about Lord Coleridge's reputation for barring students from his library and took the only possible course round it. Aunt Tim, if she knew about it, as she probably did, kept her own counsel and pretended innocence. Now she was to suffer for her intrepidity the fright of carrying a family treasure on her person.

The Royal Photographic Society sent me to Mr Huber in Red Lion Passage, a photographer using a relatively new contact printing process from Switzerland. He did a very satisfactory job, at a reasonable price, and I took the notebook early one morning on the way to the boat train, to dear Aunt Tim, and delivered it to her in her dressing gown. I can still feel the freshness of that early morning in Oxford, and the freshness of my own naiveté. 'Little did I know,' as the gothic horror novelists say, what lay in store for me with that complicated manuscript, still less what the photographing of those one hundred and twenty-three pages would lead to. For the moment the photographing meant not only that I had now, with the longhand lecture reports (typed by a professional typist thanks to a grant from St Hugh's for the purpose), and Coleridge's annotations on Tennemann, all the basic manuscripts for the editing of the Philosophical Lectures. It also meant that instead of spending days and nights making an imperfect transcript, inevitably inadequate, of S.T.Coleridge's cramped pages of notes, I could go off on a canoe trip as planned, down the length of the Wye with Thorney, a jubilant holiday before embarking for home. Never was a manuscript more luckily mislaid!

On returning home I felt the first thing I wanted to do was to write to John Livingston Lowes about the excitement and the jigsaw puzzle of the Philosophical Lectures. We had been in correspondence in August about Coleridge's reading of Josephus.

Lowes, as all Coleridgians know, made remarkable use of an early Coleridge notebook in the British Museum, one known as the Gutch Memorandum Book after its custodian, Matthew Gutch. By connecting many entries in it with *The Ancient Mariner*, *Kubla Khan* and *Christabel* and with Coleridge's reading and Dorothy Wordsworth's observations of nature, he produced *The Road to Xanadu*, *A Study in the Ways of the Imagination*, that aroused students everywhere to a new look at the romantics, in spite of T. S.Eliot. So when I was invited by that splendid Oxford hostess, Mrs Buckler, to meet Lowes at luncheon it was a very high moment. He was a tiny man with tiny hands and feet and a very mobile face; he generated so much electricity one forgot the small size of the battery. As I later told him, I would always be able to boast that I caused him to spill coffee over Mrs Buckler's beautiful Turkish rug by showing him a reference by Coleridge to the Wandering Jew—one he had looked for in vain when he was writing his book. (He could be excused for not searching STC's notes on Tennemann for it, where I pounced on it knowing he needed it.) When I pulled my little slip of paper out of my pocket and handed it to him his nervous hands shook so violently that Mrs Buckler's oriental carpet suffered. His second edition was just out. Oh, *why* had we not met before, he said. But I had only just found it. 'We must keep in close touch henceforth, then.' Out of his contagious excitement he had a way of opening up vistas. I remember biking hard round Port Meadow to work off and absorb the incredibility of our good talk together.

Thus I felt the need to write to him, in October 1933,

'. . . One thing I learned this summer which I feel I really must pass on to you for what it is worth. I think you could get into Lord Coleridge's library if you wished! I gathered from our conversation in Oxford that you thought it was a hopeless prospect.

'By an extraordinarily kind dispensation of the gods I worked on the material there again this summer and learned a good many things. My reason for thinking you would be welcome there is based partly on two conversations, (1) with Lady Coleridge, who had just received a copy of *The Road to Xanadu* and was thrilled with it. I told her a little about your lectures in Oxford (still remembered with the original enthusiasm) and about your work generally; she said she would very much like to meet you. (2) With Lord Coleridge, on the various people engaged in work on Coleridge, sympathizing with his difficulty in knowing to whom to allow access to manuscripts in the course of which he said that this man Lowes now, sounded all right, and that was different.

'If you would like to feast yourself on the fifty-five notebooks and about one hundred volumes containing marginalia in that most un-Esteccean custody I should be only too glad to give you any facts, about the MSS or other, that I have, if only to persuade you to cast that experienced and sympathetic eye over new and uncharted Coleridgian roads . . .'

Alas, Lowes was not well, and unable to go to England. Neither had he the pleasure of seeing that row of notebooks, nor have we had the benefit of what he might have done with them, though he gave me what help he could in the next few years.

I was back in England the summer of 1936, and again a guest in the Chanter's House. This time I think I really did not invite myself, though I may have done, for I was made to feel that the door was now open. Naturally there were many things I wanted to see.

Acquaintance was ripening into friendship, and perhaps this is the moment, anticipating some experiences still in the future, to record in more detail impressions of these two Coleridges whom I came to love dearly. They are two who will be very little known to fame, in comparison with the poet and the judges, and Geoffrey in particular seemed to suffer inwardly from a sense of this. Yet I wonder if any others of his direct forebears would have been so helpful to an unknown Canadian student?

Geoffrey Coleridge, though I did not know it for some years, and then mainly from relatives, had a reputation for cussedness, a tendency to say 'no' (and with a growl) rather than 'yes'. He was many times referred to as 'a bit of a character and damned difficult'. Yet it was at once apparent that he was extremely shy, and tended to bark at the world before it bit him. Like a good watchdog responsible for guarding the property, he viewed his inheritance of the Chanter's House and the estate as a trust and, I suspect, one to which, in view of his distinguished predecessors, he felt somewhat unequal. But it was a trust and he was a man of his word. He would raise beef cattle, and pinch pennies against himself, in order to leave the estate better than he found it.

He was frightened of scholars, perhaps partly because he was not proud of his Oxford pass degree, but more because he disliked the tribe of pedants and would not if he could help it endure them in his house—who could blame him? Not I, and not STC. But he pretended to hate books (except books about animals), and even more, their authors; he feared and was intolerant of the intellectual world, especially that of liberal humane studies. The arts were moving too fast for him. Our conversations were mainly about practical things—raising beef cattle, the crops, badgers, and other natural creatures. It was made the easier for me by my Canadian pioneer stock, by the summer cottage life, still close to primitive nature, where we burn oil lamps and use a wood stove and know wild animals. So it was he who proudly showed me my one and only family of badgers, and it was he who taught me how to swing a scythe to cut down thistles, a pleasant skill very useful forty years on.

I found him capable of a warmth and tenderness little suspected by his casual acquaintances. When your problem made sense to him, or even when he just had faith in you, you could depend on his allegiance.

One side I came to know was the intensity of his affection for 'Jess', to whom he was wont to refer as 'my old Trout'. At eighteen he had fallen in love with her, a girl of fourteen. Jessie was of Scottish extraction with some potent drops of Irish blood. My impression is that she was orphaned early and, according to her own accounts, brought up 'helter-skelter, a real hoyden'. She had a rather large bony frame (I had from the first moment noticed the lovely capacious hands), and a face of an extraordinary beauty, not just of feature, but born of a combined strength and vulnerability. The blend of character and sweetness, sureness and gentleness, made it evident in a moment, as Coleridge's Sara Hutchinson said of a lady's face a hundred years earlier, 'that you must love her *sometime or other.*'

Life together had not always been easy, but, by the time I knew them, here were Darby and Joan, living all their little routines as one and entertaining each other with quips and tales of their tiny adventures of the day, still after forty years deliberately setting out to charm and be charmed. Their three sons were all away, Richard in the Navy, John in the City, and James in Africa, and the great thing about being there in the Chanter's House at this time was to see them alone enjoying each other so much. He was shy about showing his feelings even here. One night after she came back from a few days' absence, he went down to the end of the garden with her to lock up the chickens. When the telephone rang I dashed out to call him. They were coming around the corner of the shrubbery arm in arm, but as he caught sight of me he pulled self-consciously aside. Her eyes—as so often—caught mine, in tender amusement.

Without Jessie Coleridge I wonder if things would have turned out for me so well. She was a woman of slender education of the most conventional ladylike kind, but she had that selfless imagination some mothers have, hard to describe without fulsomeness— the last thing she would have tolerated. The village children in Ottery St Mary loved her, and almost every other one seemed to be her godchild. At her death in 1957 her grave was strewn with scores of small bunches of primroses and violets and other April wild flowers the children had picked and put there, as well as with the choicest flowers from village gardens.

From the time our real acquaintance began, I never arrived in England without finding a welcoming letter from her, and there was always one on the eve of departure—with many more all the year round. Had I no other records I could reconstruct my personal calendar for twenty years and more from the letters written in her large unformed hand.

She could be blunt and forceful, but usually her outspokenness came out with much fun-making in between the quick nervous dashes she made at it, lest she should not spill out what she hated having to say. Her soft manner of speech, taking great care to be considerate and in so doing sometimes beating all round a subject very fast, had no mental tentativeness behind it. She was far too good a hostess and far too experienced in social grace for that. She spoke and thought with a clear-eyed intelligence and a great deal of that intuitive wisdom usually referred to as feminine. I just thought that for all the deceptive bumbling she could summon on occasion, she had brains, and the brains to conceal them. She would have flouted such an idea as utterly preposterous.

One morning a letter came to Lord Coleridge from Professor Ernest de Selincourt. He requested a visit, or rather announced his intention to come to examine the letters from Wordsworth in the Chanter's House. It sent Lord Coleridge stamping up and down the library outraged.

Who the devil was this fellow to demand the freedom of his library? He would come down Tuesday by the 2.15, would he! He could go to devil first, &c. He'd had just enough of these stupid idiots this year, wanting to snoop around. No, sir. 'Why can't they keep to their own preserves as I to mine?' &c.

Two or three days later in a calmer moment I asked and obtained, with some further caustic comments on scholars as pests, permission to transcribe for Professor de Selincourt the few Wordsworth letters there. And then something came out of my mouth that surprised me as I heard myself saying it. What made me say or think it I do not know. I had not consciously thought the thought before.

'You know, wouldn't it be a good idea to let me have a lot of this stuff photographed, to put copies in the British Museum? The notebooks anyway? Then you could send people off there.'

It had become clear that the main nuisance was personal—the library was their living room—and his dislike of having people, strangers, about.

'Such photography would cost a lot of money. You'd never be able to do it, Bookie.'

'Maybe not, but I think I might. Shall I try to find the money?'

'Well, if you like. Lot of bother. I'll just tell them to go to you-know-where. But of course—if you like. What will *you* get out of it, though?'

'Oh, I suppose I could keep one copy of the photographs for myself, and edit the notebooks from them.' Until that moment such a proposition had seemed physically and every way so impossible it had never occurred to me.

'Fancy anybody wanting to do that! You might be out enjoying the sun, girl! Oh, well—everybody's foolish one way or another, I suppose. All right. See what you can do. Certainly it did no harm to that one notebook you went off with. Get the same chap to do them.'

Naturally I had not the faintest notion of where the money was to be found for the photography. There would be about ten thousand pages to be done. In a few days I sailed for home.

It was Pelham Edgar who suggested perhaps Victoria College might and should, he thought, try to get the money for me, possibly from the Carnegie Foundation. And Dr Edward Wallace, the President, did in fact arrange for a sum of two thousand dollars to cover the cost of the photographs. (It did not cover the total cost, by any ordinary reckoning, and I learned from this experience the folly of optimistically under-estimating expenses.) When the word came in April that the grant was made, I wrote to Lord Coleridge asking him, at Mr Huber's suggestion, if he would send the notebooks up to London, so that Huber could order from Switzerland the special paper required and cut it according to the various sizes and shapes of the notebooks—a longish job owing to all the irregularities. Lord Coleridge sent them, wrapped by his own hands, without demur and with alacrity, and when I got to London in June the photographers were all set to go ahead.

I stayed at Miss Underwood's, 32 Tavistock Square, a house no longer there, swallowed up in University College; it was by all odds the best digs I ever found in London. I was short of money (having omitted room and board in the reckoning) and lived in her cheapest room on the top floor, really pretty cramped with all my gear, and not well-enough lighted, but I was very happy, and very excited by what I saw. It was difficult to keep my eye on the technicalities involved in making descriptive bibliographical notes on each notebook—watermarks, illegible and faded passages which the photographs couldn't get, and the imperfectly photographed words at

times in the inner margins when the notebook was very tightly
bound. I was working on the principle that I might never see those
notebooks again. Mr Huber was methodical and efficient, interested
enough in his job to photograph some pages twenty times where
there were problems of ink and pencil on one page, one writing
superimposed on another, and the like. He and his two lads
worked like heroes—all over the August Bank Holiday, which I
recall was very hot and shrieked for the seaside—to get finished
before I had to leave.

I went down to Oxford for the St Hugh's Gaudy and to see Mr
Kenneth Sisam of the Clarendon Press. When I had first proposed
an edition of the notebooks he said he would have to look into the
matter, as Oxford Press London already had an offer to do the
notebooks in four volumes! Upsetting, to say the least. Incredulous,
I wrote to Lord Coleridge, who replied at once, 'Find out the name
of the rogue! He has no permission from me.' So I wrote to Mr
Sisam and suggested, I suppose, that there must be some mistake,
as no one else could be using the notebooks. When I was shown
into his office he threw back his head and laughed. 'How did you,
pray, a young chit like you—colonial and all that' (turning on a
charming twinkle to which a certain kind of Englishman resorts
when he wishes with impunity to offer insults to a lady or a child)—
'and if I may say so, not meaning to be rude, a young woman too—
manage to get *that* stuff! Don't you know that England is full of
old greybeards who've been wanting to get their hands on that for
decades? Tell me. *How?*'

But an edition was what I had come to talk about, not family
gossip, especially to one who had called me a colonial. He said he
would have to consult his advisers and the Delegates. Could I send
some samples of the photographs? What exactly did I propose? I
sent a plan, and some photographs. To finish this part of the story,
though I did not know it all till years afterwards, the 'adviser' was
E. K. Chambers, who said the photographs were unreadable, i.e.
the handwriting, and that publication would entail a financial loss.
He was against it. So the Delegates turned down my proposal
on financial grounds. Chambers was writing his notoriously wrong-
headed biography of Coleridge at that time, and hating his subject.
He is reported to have said at a dinner party that he hated it so
much he did not know whether he would be able to finish it. A pity

he did, except that it became a rallying point for Coleridgians. When Mr Norrington and Mr Cumberlege, about ten years later, wished to re-open the subject of the Clarendon Press doing the Coleridge notebooks it proved impossible, because of a rule of the Delegates that anything turned down on financial grounds may not be brought up again. So that was that in Oxford. I found out from Mr Sisam that 'the rogue' was Stephen Potter, who was proposing to 'do the notebooks' from Ernest Hartley Coleridge's transcripts. I could not regret having spiked that plan, though perhaps he meant only to begin with the transcripts and eventually to get on to the originals. But Potter was unwittingly in my debt for saving him from probable madness had he tried to work from EHC's transcripts at Leatherhead. They are a compounding of STC's chaos by his own much worse one. And EHC in transcribing slid over many difficulties, much in foreign tongues, and some of the best things. But the Clarendon Press conversations were a disappointment.

Leatherhead and Gerard Coleridge presented a moment's anxiety, too, that hectic summer of '36. I went down to ask permission to borrow a handful of little notebooks I had seen there, to photograph them in the same way as the others. The vicar, kindly but sometimes irascible, was for a minute very wrathy. 'But my cousin, Lord Coleridge, had no right to give you permission to photograph or edit—the copyright is *mine*.' And he raced upstairs, the rightly proud direct descendant, to get his father's will. The will did not appear to me to clarify copyright, but anyhow, I begged his pardon for my complete ignorance of these family matters, and quickly asked if I might have his permission to photograph and edit Lord Coleridge's notebooks and his own.

'Of course you may. You have my full permission to edit. I hope you'll let me see what you do, of course. But I only want you to understand that the permission is mine to give, not his.' His father had sold the MSS to the rich Lord Chief Justice, to keep them in the family, but he had not sold the copyright! He quite sympathized with my alarm at having got the wheels of the Carnegie Corporation and Mr Huber going, only to find I was out of order. We talked a good deal about Coleridge and the notebooks, and resting comfortably back in his chair, he quoted Henry Nelson Coleridge, Coleridge's nephew and son-in-law, one of the literary executors

and an early editor, as saying that if everything STC ever wrote
were published it would all add greatly to his reputation. Mr
Coleridge made no reservations at all, and turned out all the notebooks he had—about ten altogether—for me to take to Mr Huber.

Photographing and working through the notebooks meant com-
paring every page of photograph with the originals, making notes;
it took three summer months of concentrated work, at the end of
which my spectacles needed to be stepped up considerably. It was
nerve-racking too, carrying STC's notebooks and photographs
in a briefcase every day, sleeping with them under my bed at night,
never leaving the room unlocked. Everybody told me stories of
lost briefcases—whole books lost in manuscript and never re-
covered. But finally the job was done. One copy was to go to the
British Museum, one to me. I returned the notebooks to Ottery,
staying only a night or two. As we unpacked them I began to check
them off on a list. Lord Coleridge would have none of it, and returned them to their top shelf in the newspaper wrappings I had
tied around them. (The next time I went to Ottery, nine years later,
after the war, I myself took the newspaper wrappings off and put
them back on the shelf in order.)

It was Lady Coleridge who protested that if one copy was going
to the BM what was to prevent 'some rascal' from 'skimming the
cream' and getting out a volume while my work was in progress?
So it was agreed that a letter should accompany the photographs
making it a condition that no one might publish from them until
my edition was out. Lord Coleridge and I both signed it, I think.
Anyway, he did, with a good deal of banter about the cleverness of
'my old lady—far ahead of you, Bookie'; the Director of the
Museum in acknowledging the gift accepted the condition.

The photographs were hardly unpacked in my study in Toronto
before I had a visit from an American scholar. He came from the
Middle West to check a few readings, he said. He offered himself as
joint editor of the notebooks. He had heard from Gerard Coleridge
in Leatherhead, perhaps, or some other, that I had broached the
Ottery defences and that I had permission to edit the lot. I showed
him what he asked to see and more, found him knowledgeable
about factual biographical matters, but could sense very little common ground between us when I tried to touch on philosophy or
poetry. His proposal to help with the editing seemed a bit odd, as

he did not know me nor I him. He offered the services of his wife and about a dozen graduate students—all more than a little alarming to one who had just spent a hard summer torn between the agony of getting the text of the notebooks and the bibliographical facts recorded clearly, and the ecstasies of intellectual excitement and aesthetic pleasure from the content. I was not ready to make decisions on procedures and mechanics, nor did I begin to know how the work on such tangled skeins might be divided. The evident close relations between one notebook and another, not only in dates, but in recurrent themes and ideas, were haunting me— multiple links to be quietly perceived and cautiously sorted out. The gentleman was older than I, and more experienced, though some of my encounters with his work *vis-à-vis* the manuscripts had not been such as altogether to reassure me. Still, the job ahead of me was a large one, and help, I felt, should not be lightly dismissed; on the other hand, any unsuccessful co-operation would breed difficulties that could become a major hindrance. In this uncomfortable uncertainty I asked the advice of two of my most senior colleagues—Pelham Edgar himself, and John Robins. We all went out together to a disastrous lunch. Conversation initiated by the visitor got off on more than one wrong foot. I recall, as symptomatic of the differences in style and temper of my guests, that the modest, rather solemn stranger ordered sausages and began to ask Pelham's opinion of something to do with the YMCA. Pelham looked fiercely into the menu and turned to me.

'I say, my dear, are you paying for this lunch? Because I see there's lobster . . .' Edgar's sophistication was natural and his elegance of manner had behind it at times a shrewd, mischievous sense of occasion.

'I'm having lobster, too,' I said. What John Robins ate I do not recall, but he was equally disconcerted by the conversation. The notebooks were not discussed, and all the little literary or philosophical fires we three attempted to light guttered out one after another.

Over the changing of plates for dessert, while kindly Robins engaged the visitor, Pelham Edgar looked at me and shook his head in a decided negative. We never discussed the subject of the proposal again. I got out of it, without undue awkwardness, simply because it came unreasonably early for me to be expected to answer it. A few days later Edgar said, 'I hope you are keeping a detailed diary of all your doings and conversations, especially with the Coleridges. Otherwise you will forget a good deal.' I took his advice.

Since this is a record of the facts as I remember them, another episode connected with the photographs must be set down. The Carnegie grant was to Victoria College, and the College was responsible to the corporation for an account of it. It was stated in my original letter of application that one copy of the photographs would go to the BM and one was to be permitted by Lord Coleridge to me, for editorial purposes. But Dr Brown, the Principal, thought that my set of photographs should belong to the College, and wished me to sign a statement to that effect; if I died, or left the College *for any reason*, the photographs would remain in the library. This I refused to do. The copy was not College property, I said, but mine, on a kind of editorial trust from the Coleridge family, and if I left the College I would still go on editing Coleridge. Quite another document was signed. I would leave the photographs to the College on my death.

Without dwelling on this single unpleasant episode in the history of the Coleridge enterprise and Victoria College, it may be as well to add that though the contention itself was brief enough, it betokened part of the attitude of the Principal to the status of women. I do not know whether it delayed my promotion but my intransigence certainly did not facilitate it. Already three years before, the Principal had said he would never appoint a woman to the permanent staff of the College. In fairly short order three men, with no more experience or academic qualifications, received permanent appointments over my head, and against outspoken protests from members of the Board. This, though at times hard to take, and financially unfair, did not deeply disturb me. Professionally it was serious, but not for me personally. As a junior I sat on no committees and had the minimum of examining and other departmental chores. I could escape at the first possible moment at the end of term, only to return at the latest possible moment in the fall. I could get on with my work.

Dr Brown's well-known anti-feminism—women students who graduated in the thirties will remember his homilies on woman's place being in the home—led to an unforgotten conversation with the first Dean of Women at Victoria, Margaret Addison. Long after her retirement she came to dine with me one night in Annesley Hall, to discuss an offer of a teaching post in Japan which she was keen that I should take. It seemed to me too far away from the British Museum and the Coleridge manuscripts, but it was tempting in various other ways. The night was a clear October or November one, and Miss Addison loved to scuffle the dry fallen leaves with her big broad feet; we went out for a walk round and round about in Queen's Park, weighing pros and cons. Finally I said,

'You know, Dr Brown has said he will not appoint permanently any woman to teach men, and yet, I still feel inclined to forget Japan and stick with Victoria. I want to teach Canadian students and I love this place. It has shown faith in me.' I agreed in general with the theory that one ought to leave one's *alma mater*. But something—maybe the Irish—made me pause. So I said to Miss Addison, 'After all, Dr Brown is only *one* mortal man.'

Long silence, long strides, for perhaps a quarter of a mile.

'Well, dear,' she said with that complete finality of which she was capable, 'if you see it that clearly, and are prepared to fight it out, I would like to see you stay. I'll tell you this,' she gave a shocked chuckle at having the thought, 'time is on your side.' Time was. Dr Brown *was* mortal. The war, too, helped women to recognition. But I have sometimes thought, in spite of the manifest objections, that there were certain advantages in being a downtrodden female scholar with no permanent status for the first fourteen years of teaching. Rapid advancement has prices I did not have to pay.

III

1937–1946

The notebooks were now photographed. The next step was to transcribe them. I also needed to talk to experienced Coleridgians about what would be required in a useful edition of the notebooks. Coleridgians, as I have suggested, were scarce. Certainly there were none in Canada, and few anywhere. Harvard had a little manuscript material and a few annotated books I needed to make myself aware of, so I wrote again to Lowes. It was an exciting visit in ways unexpected as well as hoped for.

Lowes was kindness itself. I found the little bird-like figure with his bright quick eyes and eager intense face as he waited on the steps of the Widener Library, at once full of questions about the notebooks. I had taken him transcriptions of a few passages I knew would delight him, and now he shared as fully with me. Good Coleridgians, like Coleridge himself, do not hold back. He took me to his study and showed me an aged steamer trunk nearly full of his papers: scribblers, filing folders, clippings, all notes he said for his projected edition of that early so-called 'Gutch notebook' in the British Museum, of which he had made Sherlock Holmes use in *The Road to Xanadu*. I asked him if he would like to edit all seventy notebooks, and he in turn offered to share his notes on the one he had been working on so long. He was too involved with other things to accept my suggestion, and beginning to distrust his memory too much; and perhaps he guessed too well the extent of the task. His most prized possession was Coleridge's annotated copy of Donne's *LXXX Sermons*. His hands trembled as he turned the pages, also his voice. I remember as we discussed some notebook entries in which Coleridge referred to prayer and its difficulties he turned to the volume of Donne in front of him and read, quaveringly:

'That soule, that is accustomed to direct her selfe to God upon every occasion, that, as a flowre at Sun-rising, conceives a sense

of God in every beame of his, and spreads and dilates it selfe towards him in a thankfulnesse in every small blessing that he
sheds upon her; . . . that soule, who, whatsoever string be
strucken in her, base or treble, her high or her low estate, is
ever tun'd toward God, that soule prayes sometimes when it
does not know that it prayes.'

We also talked of Helen Waddell, who had encouraged him to
edit the Gutch notebook. He loved her work; another bond between us was our enthusiasm for her *Mediaeval Latin Lyrics* and
The Wandering Scholars. He knew of riches to come as I did not,
but later I was to get in touch with her about him.

After three or four days of such pleasures, my return home was
suddenly cancelled by a hurricane that hit the New England coast.
In the early afternoon a gust in Harvard Yard ripped off my brown
straw hat, to my embarrassment, for Lowes was bound to chase it.
The next minute I was chasing his brown felt porkpie. The comic
effect was about even, for as we noted on exchanging hats, we
neither of us had dropped our Coleridge-stuffed brief-cases. Later
in the afternoon I stood in my room in a student boarding house
in Arlington Street listening to the fire-reels and ambulances and
sirens between the roars of the wind, and watching great elms
blow down across the roofs of cars parked in the street, carrying
with them electric and telephone lines and poles. Warnings were
sent over the radio and by loudspeakers in the streets of the danger
from live electric wires down everywhere. I wondered if the big
wooden house I was staying in would stand. I saw the window of a
dress shop ripped out, and racks of dresses as if on roller skates
blown out in every direction. By evening things calmed down and
curiosity and hunger for the evening meal took one out into the
muggy heat. The streets as shopkeepers sorted out their goods
among the ruins looked like a badly organized rummage sale.
Floods had also done immense damage. Railway bridges and cul-
verts were washed out, and the railway lines between Cambridge,
Mass. and Toronto were awash.

I met Lowes next day in the library. He reassured his bank
that it was safe to cash my cheque for the money I needed for
the four or five extra days before return was possible via Montreal. After a long tedious night in a hot sleeping car, Montreal,

with its crisp October air, had never seemed so exhilarating.

In 1938 and 1939, less during term and more during the summers, I began transcribing, for it could be carried on in the intervals of teaching, lecture preparation, and the pleasures of summer cottage life.

Transcribing was more exacting work than one might think, but the pleasures of these first journeys through this extraordinary mental landscape were sharp and unpredictable. Notebook 1 begins suitably enough with three conundrums, and an entry on the derivation of the word *smile* linked with infant speech and Greek and German consonants. Then follows this fantasy: 'Cities amid the ruins of the world like cottages in some Castle ruined.' Sometimes the physical tussle simply to read was like trying to pull a juniper root out of our granite rocks. For example, there were the pencilled notes taken down illicitly in the dark in the gallery of the House of Commons during Pitt's speeches in 1800 on the war with France, notes worked up in the *Morning Post* next day into better speeches than Pitt delivered, it was said. Some entries were difficult because of the impossibility of anticipating Coleridge's vocabulary; some passages written in or about emotional difficulties with Wordsworth, or Sara Hutchinson, or Mrs Coleridge, or Southey, presented every sort of obstacle, including bits of cipher. But the rewards were legion, whether he described objects—the eye of a lizard, water in a hundred aspects, a painting by Washington Allston, or states of mind—'Foul stream, House of Commons' Consciences', or more personally, 'the hard-heartedness of healthy people', or the difference between love and desire.

The many literary entries, comments on Milton, Jeremy Taylor and a hundred others, certain Germans and Italians, were sometimes highly elliptical, erratic, sometimes borrowed without trace; in fact many quotations were anonymous. But one striking fact about the entries having to do with writers and thinkers was that, whatever his attitude, the relationship to them was intimate, real, a shared inheritance, a felt intellectual drive; he sought a common climate even with opponents. Whether a scientist or philosopher or poet lived yesterday or five hundred yesterdays ago made no difference when ideas were up for assessment; the ages might advance in knowledge but temperament, undimmed by time, was taken into account. The moral reputation of Epicurus was as dear

to him as Wordsworth's. To transcribe Coleridge was to be introduced to a timeless international society of great minds, whether
he discussed their ideas on the largest scale or pounced hawk-like
on a lurking fallacy. To transcribe the notebooks was no slavery.

As transcription proceeded, numerous decisions had to be
made. I have elsewhere described the chaos of the notebooks; in
fact they were chaos seventy times over, one in each notebook.
They had been used from front to back and back to front, sometimes over many years with great gaps—as much as twenty-three
years between two entries on one page; some pages were written
over twice, for two different purposes, ink written over pencil;
pages were left blank or accidentally missed and later returned to;
extraneous leaves were inserted within notebooks, in one case notebooks within a notebook; writing was done in every conceivable
situation—desk, stage-coach, crouching for shelter from the rain
under a mountain rock, on horseback, on shipboard, in bed. It was
often difficult to tell where one entry ended and another began,
especially if the medium remained constant for a few pages,
whether it was pen, pencil, crayon, or red gout-medicine.

How was such chaos to be presented intelligibly in print? It was
clear that other readers besides myself would like to know not
only the dates and chronological pattern of entries but also what
was on a page. When in 1812 Coleridge picked up an old notebook
of 1800 and jotted down an entry on a blank half-page, what else
did he see there? What associations were set up by memoranda he
found there of a decade or so earlier? The physical relation of
entries must be shown, as well as the time-sequence. The notebooks having been assigned numbers, probably by Ernest Hartley
Coleridge, the grandson, the numbering of entries within them
could be designated, for instance, 1.1–1.26 in Notebook 1, a notebook of twenty-six entries; in Notebook 21, of over three hundred
entries, 21.1–21.367. Two ledgers were set up, one for listing
entries notebook by notebook, assigning conjectural dates where
none existed; the other was a monthly calendar, on which dated
and datable entries were entered as the information was filled in.
Slowly the chronological series built up the time-sequence, and, by
means of the notebook-tables, the spatial physical content of each
notebook, page by page, could be seen. The procedure in the main
was simple enough, but it had to be evolved out of the nature of

the materials themselves, there being no precedent that I knew of for such a dual presentation. It has been gratifying to see that the system works, and to know that it has become usefully applicable to notebooks of other authors.

I was extremely fortunate in the transcribing to have the services of a college classmate, Marion Forward, as typist. A clever woman of very modest ambition, she had begun her career in the depression typing index cards in Norwegian in the Department of Botany, knowing neither the language, the subject, nor the technical terms, and hence she developed the skill that comes of reading closely and precisely, letter by letter. She was an ideal typist for Coleridge, meeting his unexpected vocabulary and his German, Latin, and Italian (everything but his Greek) without a quiver. In fact, after struggling with my transcriptions (with the photographs beside her) for some months, it became mortifyingly clear that she could read Coleridge's writing almost as readily as she could read mine. When I had sorted out the division of entries, she gradually took over the first draft of the transcribing, and did it superbly. Gaps of illegibility, cancelled words, faint pencil, or very difficult passages were inevitably left for me, and often for consultation in England of the manuscripts themselves. Incredibly, perhaps, it is the case that up to the very last stages of the page-proofs a fresh glimpse sometimes may bring a fresh reading. No one who has not experienced similar problems will credit how easy it is to read absurdly wrong, how difficult, with complete assurance, to read absolutely right. Marion called me at midnight during some crisis and said in a voice shaking with awe and alarm, 'What you read as *Dorothy* I read as *Hartley*. Are we going mad?' The reading was so debatable I had to consult the actual notebook again on the next trip to England, as it happened, years later.

The summer vacation in Canadian universities, originally based on the farmers' need of student help with the harvest, was long— about three and a half months. That is a practical length of time for study abroad, or to make attractive the thought of a permanent summer retreat nearer home for the purpose. After a summer's exploring of various Georgian Bay islands still available as 'Crown Land', that is, never yet privately owned, Jessie Macpherson, a colleague in Victoria College, and I found island B578, some sixteen miles south-west of Parry Sound. We bought it for $187.78

—five and half acres of granite rock with a fine mixture of white pine, silver birch, oak, maple, hemlock, spruce, poplar, cedar, pin-cherry and other trees. We chose it for its beauty of varied shoreline and surface, and for its setting. To the west, except for a few slivers of rock, the open bay; north and south, channels between islands upon islands upon islands, which eastwards join with the mainland of the pre-Cambrian shield. We chose it also for its livability. Its north shore provides a comforting horseshoe-shaped harbour for small boats in any weather, and to the south and west are three little coves with sandy bottoms—beautiful and private swimming pools.

On the sixth of May, 1939, with cakes of ice floating about, we took out Johnson Tabobandung of the Parry Island band of Ojibwa, and an architect friend, Forrest Telfer, to mark out the cottage site and advise about our own rough general plan. The very rocks seemed ice-bound. The only green was the evergreen of pine, spruce, cedar, and the ubiquitous juniper stretching across the rocks. Johnson's evident pleasure in our choice of island, and our instant unanimity as to the cottage site, is still a shining moment in the mind's eye. In a Parry Sound hotel we all signed a contract for the building which was to be completed by June 15—Johnson's estimate of the time he would need. I like to boast on behalf of my Indian friends that it was in fact built only four days behind schedule (two of which were days of pouring rain).

When Johnson told us they had the roof on, about June first, we went up for the week-end. Laughter rippled round the rafters as the men worked; it would die down for a bit while the hammers pounded, and then a little high-pitched giggle or a few words in Ojibwa would set it going again. Chipmunks were everywhere, rearing their little ones, and resenting the intrusive building. They scolded noisily. The Indians teased them. They also sang hymns. The best carpenter was a Salvation Army captain named Partridge, whose stout figure could be seen on Saturday nights and Sundays in Parry Sound in his huge Salvation Army uniform with dignity leading the Sallies. He had learned his excellent carpentry in the shipyards on the Great Lakes during the first Great War.

I am proud to relate, too, that when Johnson's Indian workmen left the island, the surplus pieces of lumber were piled neatly under the house, papers picked up and rubbish burned, and the only sign of workmen having been about was a few blackened stones, at a distance from the house under a sheltering rock, against which they had built a small fire to make their tea. After a few years had passed I turned the inconspicuous little recess into a memorial by planting a fern there.

By the natural processes of friendship, inevitably slow in the first thirty years over a cultural divide, Johnson and Christina Tabobandung and their family, and others too, on the Parry Island Reserve, became a highly-valued part of our lives. They opened and closed the cottage each season, they installed the pump and repaired it, endlessly they cut and delivered and piled hundreds of cords of wood for our stove and fireplace. They brought, when they happened to think of it, our mail, for to this island there is no road, no postman, no newspaper, no telephone.

Johnson, with an acute and painful sense of an Ojibwa culture in danger of passing away, would occasionally talk about conflicts— in the advice he had from his grandparents, between old and young on the reserve—or express worries over his own people, his own family.

Johnson and his family one summer brought to the island their mourning. When their eldest son joined the army they were grieved enough, but when Percy, the much loved second son, was drowned, sorrow crushed them. Drowned, or killed in a quarrel? The question haunted us all, and night after still summer night, for a week or more, from various places the family converged, on the west porch Percy had helped to build. It was impossible to forget Coleridge's lines on 'Three Sorts of Friends', Ac-, Con-, and In-quaintances,

> 'But for Inquaintance I know only two,
> The friend I've mourned with, and the maid I woo'.

Johnson brought also his great pot-bellied rising and falling laughter, together with his own sane perspective on things. Having helped to carry up twenty crates or more of books one year, he tossed his farewell advice over his shoulder, 'Don't you girls forget to lie under a tree sometimes.'

Our first summer on the island, the last of the summers between the wars, was a singularly beautiful one, and though we were full of house-guests, it gave a tremendous fillip to my work. Jessie was writing a PhD thesis and reading G.E.Moore intensively; she was no Coleridgian and gave me many a battle. I was trying to relate Coleridge's notebook-materials to his prose works and letters, and to grasp the purpose behind many entries.

We decided that to avoid the seductions of these lovely days it would be essential to have a routine. Come fair, come foul weather, guests, or other eventualities, we would work four hours each morning till lunch-time and knock off for various active pleasures only in the afternoons. 'Mrs Mac', Jessie's mother, co-operated quietly and efficiently, though ours was not the kind of more boisterious social summer cottage life she had known in her youth. She was a splendid cook, and she loved the Bay. So it all worked, and in this happy household Coleridge strode on apace.

News of the world, though we got it irregularly (no transistor radios then), was growing very dark by August 1939. The launch driver who came to take Jessie and her mother back to town greeted us gruffly. 'A big ship's been sunk. They say four hundred Canadians on board.' It was the *Athenia*, and for us the beginning of the War. We knew that many of our colleagues were on her.

That same dire launch brought also, by one of these strange ironical synchronicities, a letter from Germany, from my old friend Herr Max von Ruperti, now retired and in Göttingen with access to a good library. He had lost his job, but fortunately not his head, when Hitler took power in 1933. I had asked him the source for a seven-line German quip, one of Coleridge's notebook entries, about the Lord of Plesse, and here came his answer, in a letter full of sadness at the condition of Europe, but of course not aware when he wrote in August that disaster was so imminent. It was a ghastly, but also in some way a comforting, reminder that the human elements transcend what Coleridge called 'all our dainty terms for fratricide'. My thoughts and heart-sinkings (all too justified) flew to Ruperti's two sons, both of military age.

I was staying another ten days in September to work before closing the cottage, but at least four of those days were spent mostly chopping wood to control the turmoil of thoughts—of England, and English friends, of German friends, of the inevitable destruction everywhere, of the calamitous inhumanity of man unleashed on the world.

I was to have had a term's leave beginning in September. At one stroke it was cancelled and my lecture load almost doubled, owing to the enlistment of men from the department. Although we felt our geographical remoteness from falling bombs, fire-watching, and severe rationing, and though we suffered chiefly by identification with those who were directly touched, yet the war coloured daily life by imposing all sorts of strange activities and obligations. I found myself looking for domestic work for some scores of German women whose husbands had been suddenly interned; some of them were pro-Nazi but most of them knew little of what it was all about. They only knew that their provider was gone and that they had little or no English, no training, and no livelihood. A committee was formed to help them to navigate; we hoped thus to minimize hatreds. They were difficult people, and not less so in their real difficulties. Then came the English war-guest children, sometimes with mothers. College buildings were a temporary clearing station. Flats, furniture, clothing, groceries had to be found, and many problems had to be solved. Then there came the Japanese Canadians from the Pacific Coast—a shoddy episode in which hundreds of loyal Canadian subjects were suddenly scooped up into makeshift detention camps in the interior. Losing their farms, industries and businesses, often to predatory competitors, they were brought eastwards, dissemination being considered the safest policy. We were asked to find employment for them, and to help them settle in strange surroundings.

By this time the Civil Liberties Association, which had concerned itself *inter alia* with the civil rights of these displaced persons, was consuming most of my spare time. It was politically fascinating, highly educational, and at times great fun of a contentious sort. It seemed also a thoroughly Coleridgian *Watchman*-like activity.

Another extra during the war years was extension lecturing one night a week, replacing one of the men on duty elsewhere. This meant twenty lectures on English grammar and composition, designed for adults who for various reasons had had to abandon their formal education early, and who wished to improve their security in English. They were often interesting persons, discussion was lively, and I perforce studied English grammar as I never had done before. They asked fundamental questions for which answers had to be found. Undoubtedly the best way to learn a subject is to teach it, and I enjoyed and was grateful to those classes, though about halfway through each winter I wondered if they were worth the preparation of exercises, the loss of one evening in seven, and the long icy treks across the campus in zero weather—all for ten dollars a night I often longed to spend on the notebooks. These times were lively too. Some of the students in my house got the idea our telephone was being tapped because of my Civil Liberties activities, and so they would telephone me from another line and carry on outrageously subversive conversations, so ludicrous that even the dullest Dogberry on the police force must have been entertained.

Looking back, it is difficult to imagine how one got through all those tightly-packed days. Sometimes in term there were as many as twenty-two hours a week of undergraduate lectures to give, many of them on new courses never undertaken before, with all the thousand other ills that academics are heir to, before one could even begin to think of individual students and their needs. Living in a college residence one sees those needs at close range. But just as it is valuable to be tantalized, so can it also be useful to be interrupted—to drop a thing in mid-sentence. On coming back to it one finds the groove. One is pulled along to complete the sentence; the initiative is already taken, one need not begin cold. In time this suspension was to become almost a technique—an aid to energy, in part the making a virtue of necessity as teaching and administrative chores, the practical needs of family life and every day, broke in on writing. One began to realize that these irrelevancies to the work should not be eliminated—if unresented they can whet the appetitite and sharpen the knife. One needs also some periods free of them—but I have come to think that these free stretches serve one most richly when the cluttered ones have been somehow endured with the muscles flexed.

However, after the strenuousness of the months from September to May, I made a dash for Georgian Bay and recuperation, with what dregs of energy remained. In the first wartime summer I planted a vegetable garden, which everyone said was ridiculous on that bare granite rock. But as the old supply boat had stopped running, it was worth a try, sixteen miles away from a shop. There was little or no depth of soil, except in a few crevices, but by carrying earth and dead leaves and wood fibre we did get three tiny garden plots of very rich soil. So rich, and so forced by the heat of the rocks, that by planting about May 24th (the earliest frost-free date) we had by July 15th beans, lettuces, spinach, vegetable marrows, carrots, beets, tomatoes, most of the vegetables we needed —fresh from the garden to the pot.

Seven island summers were incredibly lovely in themselves, but no island is an island in wartime. It is not easy to pinpoint the margins of enjoyment and anxiety. There was a degree of peace and quiet and comfort that can make one feel guilty at any time, in wartime positively wicked. I stretched out on a great elephant-back of smooth grey pre-Cambrian granite, feeling the permanency of this oldest exposed piece of the earth's surface, and knowing that half a world away the world, our cultural world, was tumbling down. Whole cities were being devastated. Students we had admired were being killed, and students we were teaching now were waiting their turn and time. In Europe, Jews and liberals were being imprisoned and rumours of concentration camps were too sinister to be believed. We felt cut off from active physical participation by the Atlantic, by being the wrong age and sex. Yet we clung to the thought that it was never more important to be teaching, and to hold steadfast, for the young as well as for one's own dynamics, to this commitment to the basic values. It was often difficult to maintain clarity.

Coleridge helped. In the early notebooks, on which I was chiefly working, there were the seeds of his early attacks on Pitt's war against the French, and the germs of *The Watchman*, the motto of which, 'That All may know the Truth and that the Truth may make us *FREE*', is also the motto over the doorway of Victoria College. The notebooks were in fact rich in relevance to our situation.

This, then, was a period of slow osmosis, of transcribing, dating, absorbing, digesting, relating the notebook entries to his letters and published works. The days were full of Coleridge's flashes of lightning, at times too full of excitement to work sitting down, at times infuriating or agonizing. The great thing was having time in these early stages, and the freedom from distraction, for an absorption process that had to be more than merely cerebral.

Jessie's presence was powerful and positive, though she had little notion of it herself. With a clear head and a gifted easy way of organizing life around her, she quietly set the style of our days: the early-morning swim, the good breakfasts cooked on the wood stove, her brown bread, the regular satisfying rhythms of work; then the afternoon explorations of the islands by canoe, or reading luxuriously far afield, music from an old wind-up gramophone, argument arising often from the *Canadian Forum* or the *New Statesman*, the occasional entertaining of neighbours or house-guests.

Jessie loved wrestling with tough mental exercises. One night she had been fascinated by some mathematical problem, and finally went to bed defeated. It was a peaceful black night round our screened porch, good for sleeping, but suddenly I wakened to hear Jessie leaping out of her bed and making for the living-room, with a flashlight, and her book. 'I think I've got it!' she was saying to herself. Among the tender recollections of those years is Jessie practising scales and exercises in her rich mezzo voice, out on the rocks on the south shore. Almost always there was some Bach, often out of the *St Matthew Passion*. 'Have mercy, Lord, on me,' she sang, and meant it.

Often deeply depressed, miserably unsure of herself in ways the world was not allowed to see, she had nevertheless a quick un-vindictive wit that spilled out to surprise even those who best knew her. She was a splendid piece of dignity to live with and our lives on the island had just that mixture of intellectual *frisson* and deep affection necessary to a friendship as secure as the granite rock on which it was built.

As the war went on and on, seeming endless, and it was clearly not possible to do final editorial work on the notebooks with the Atlantic between me and the original manuscripts, I began to think again about the Philosophical Lectures, for which I had more nearly complete materials. I had the verbatim reports of twelve of the fourteen lectures, Coleridge's lecture notes for all fourteen of them, and the sourcebook he used for his facts, Tennemann's *Geschichte der Philosophie* with his marginalia on ten of the volumes, and some other odds and ends of manuscript material collected earlier in the British Museum. So part of the summers of '43 and '44 and '45 were spent on the lectures.

For recreation at this time I began to write *The Grandmothers*, until I found it riding me too hard. I had long wished to write something about my paternal grandmother, the pioneering one, but each attempt was abandoned, from self-criticism and shyness.

Then during the war Hanna Fischl told me of her Czech grandmother, and the close parallel suggested the possibility of something between truth and fiction. The Fischls provided the Czech
background, the Czech songs, the Czech food. The Canadian part
of the story gave me the excuse for tramping the hills of Mulmur
and reliving The Fenian Raids. It was a rest from Coleridge, and
from the war, and I loved doing it.

IV

1946–1947

Though the war was over, shipping in the summer of 1946 was still strictly controlled, passages to Britain being granted on but two grounds, compassion and business. I could put forward no sensible pleas for compassion, and at first sight Coleridge did not look like an urgent commercial proposition. However, nothing ventured, nothing gained. I had had a letter from Charles Madge, literary editor at that time of the young Pilot Press, asking me if it were the case, as he had heard in the British Museum, that I was editing the Coleridge notebooks and whether I would consider the Pilot Press as publisher. There was also Cambridge University Press, which in 1937 had postponed discussion but had left the door ajar; after Oxford rejected Coleridge and me I had gone to Cambridge. That wise old Johnsonian S.C. Roberts had looked me up and down with a kindly twinkle in his eye and told me to come back when I was ready with more specific proposals as to the method and style and extent of my edition. There was also Blackwell, rumoured to be planning a complete edition of Coleridge's works. Fortified with correspondence from these, I persuaded the Canadian shipping authority that the publishing world was crying out for Coleridge, and that in the national economic rehabilitation I should have a commercial passage.

The *Cavina* was formerly a banana-boat running between Bristol and the West Indies. Her capacity was a hundred and forty passengers, and we had a hundred and thirty nine, all of us quite secondary to some sort of steel bars, wood-blocks, and paper goods —no bananas or other luxuries. There were no deck-chairs, but we had good hot sunny days in June sitting on the deck floor, herded together, an interesting group of persons with definite purposes in crossing. There were a few wonderful old people whose grounds were obviously the compassionate ones; the one I best remember was a wiry ninety-year-old granny who taught us what a 'flannelfoot' was (brandy and milk) and drank a double every night before dinner. We had also the detective from Scotland Yard who had tracked down Fred Rose, the disguised communist spy turned Canadian MP; two archaeologists going to Burma; a professor of political science from Toronto; and a bewildered businessman who had made and lost three fortunes, spoke six or eight languages, and was in general pathetically forlorn. The most memorable conversation I had on board was with the grim old Irish baggage-man on the last night, who confided sourly that he had 'passed through all the extremes of vice and virtue', leaving me pretty unclear as to where he was, morally speaking, at that moment. Wherever it was, he was certainly not happy. As we sailed across the Irish sea to Liverpool, the ship's captain, entertaining with cocktails before lunch, rushed out to the bridge. We were passing his house on Islandmagee, where his wife, a rosy soncy body, was out waving her apron in greeting. He hooted back. Phyllis Bedells did an Irish jig for us, I remember: she was, I believe, the first English ballerina to come out to help train the Winnipeg ballet.

The first post-war summer in England was a time to reckon with in itself. In fact I kept a diary of a kind and thought of doing something with it, but Coleridge was in the van of my thoughts and other people were writing about 'the condition of England', 'bloody but unbowed'. No visit ever again has had such rich or nostalgic or awe-inspiring moments, simply in the streets, and naturally there were personal contexts also. And there were some highly entertaining ones, like being referred to resentfully by two businessmen opposite me at lunch upstairs in the Bull and Mouth, scarcely *sotto-voce*, as 'the aftermath of the war'. And the notice in the Balliol College porter's lodge: 'Gentlemen under eighteen years may call at the Bursar's office for their banana.' Less amusing, on a temporary hoarding I saw a printed notice:

Names of MPs
Voting for Bread
Rationing
in the
Commons on Thursday
Will be published here as
Public Enemies and Dictators

The linden trees were in bloom and London that June was sunny. The parks were as beautiful as ever, and the British Museum guards as cordial, and one was glad to see so many of the same ones still extant. The British Museum itself was frigid and clammy. No heat during the war, and as July and August got wetter and wetter the walls almost ran water. I kept on adding each morning another layer of woollen clothing. A direct hit had wiped out certain sections of books, as the returned slips told us: 'Destroyed by enemy action.' The newspapers were now in Colindale, but many other treasures that had been rusticated for the duration were back and available. It is one of the special pleasures of a researcher's life to go to a great library (and the British Museum is for English studies the greatest) generally secure of finding the right books with the answers to a list of problems unsolved elsewhere, to see the guesses confirmed (or denied in favour of the unexpected) and to see problems coming full circle.

The *Philosophical Lectures* began to take final shape, and I began to talk to publishers. I had good sessions with Charles Madge. He had caught the Coleridge fire at Cambridge from I.A.Richards. The Pilot Press was very new and, except for Madge, un-English, and there were disquieting rumours about it. Blackwell did not conceal his distaste for it, but then he also ran down Coleridge, the publication of most notebooks ('rag-bags'), and women as scholars and editors—all with smiling affability. He wanted the Notebooks, but oh yes, of course they would do the *Philosophical Lectures* first if they were ready and if I insisted. Would I care to have the use of a room upstairs and the services of their top man on Coleridge, William King? There was a weird session with Sir somebody, whose name now escapes me, who was to be the editor of their proposed collected edition. I had never heard of him and suspected from the expression on his face that he had only just heard of Coleridge. Was he to be front man to save the firm from having an independent female editor? I couldn't make it out. The plan was a recent concoction, I thought, no other editors having been named for specific works. I felt no real literary concern or point of view about editing Coleridge. Even in practical matters the atmosphere was disquieting. What about the American rights and editions? I had heard of authors unhappy about this aspect. I was told by an eminent Oxford don that sometimes financial statements were difficult to get hold of, that there tended to be unconcern about review copies going out, &c, &c; one hears such gossip often enough, but there was a lot of it, and I was young, green, and scared. Blackwell showed me some of his Shakespeare Head editions as a sample of his work, clearly keen to capture the Notebooks; but there was the utmost off-handedness about the complexities of the manuscripts, even about my preparation of a typescript for type-setting. No terms were discussed, no contract offered—all a very gentlemanly sort of thing—yet I felt, rightly or wrongly, a tight-fisted tradesman spirit underneath. The atmosphere was nineteenth century, in the publisher's interest, not in Coleridge's.

To go up to London again to Madge and the Pilot Press was to step into the twentieth century and, into keenness and awareness of why Coleridge was still alive and why we must publish him. So I signed two contracts with them, one for the *Philosophical Lectures* and, later, one for another book of more general interest, a result of our conversations. I had rambled on about Coleridge's prose, how it could yield many passages which would display those prophetic observations that make him startlingly contemporary with us in various fields—logic, education, psychology, social criticism, language. 'Do it!' they said. 'It will help perhaps to cover the loss on the *Philosophical Lectures*, which will *not* sell.' This became *Inquiring Spirit*, but in the event not published by the Pilot Press.

The summer of 1946 was exciting from other causes than signing contracts; the research itself would have created excitement enough, but in the Coleridge story another crucial moment occurred, appropriately in Ottery St Mary, at the railway station.

It had been a particularly choice visit with the Coleridges. After the long blank stretch of the war, they were in a new way eagerly responsive to the world outside. What did Canada think about England now, was the question generally asked among the English, who in my student days of the thirties, before the war and the arrival of Canadian airmen, troops, and wartime food parcels, sometimes gave the impression that they couldn't care less about what Canada thought about anything. In 1946 I found the Chanter's House with only part-time daily help, and the two old dears clearing their own table and doing their own washing-up. Lord Coleridge disappeared quickly from the scullery the first night the moment I picked up a tea towel. Lady Coleridge told me of a titled friend declining their invitation to visit for a few days because she said she had firmly resolved, after several experiences, that she 'would *not* go visiting from sink to sink'. Many small episodes were sharp indicators of the creeping little miseries of the war. Every kitchen scrap was saved, not for pigs any more but for chickens now, and Lord Coleridge enquired daily as to the number of eggs. She was exuberant about having got a bag of meal for the hens from a grocer she did not deal with, through the gardener. Geoffrey went out to shoot a rabbit for food for the old dog. And could she spare him just a *little* more hot water in the mornings for washing and shaving? Fuel was scarce. Evacuees had recently left the house (some invalids and their nurses who handed Lady Coleridge fundamentalist religious tracts when they passed her on the stairs), all but the nursery school which still appeared in the mornings; and there were still many signs of wartime activities and philanthropies about the place.

Much in the wind these days was a campaign for funds to restore the Ottery church bells. The largest of these beautiful bells had been discovered to have a crack in it, and I think part of the fabric of the tower was in need of repair, so the bell was taken down, lest it fall or be hit by enemy bombs.

'I suppose you've read what your old poet wrote about those bells, Bookie? "The poor man's only music", didn't he say? Well, you see we are taking care of them.'

In fact the dates of my visit had been fixed to coincide with the village fête, August 3, when the Chanter's House and the gardens would be thrown open to the public, conducted tours two shillings and sixpence towards the bells fund. I was dragooned into service as a guide, and had to pass an examination on the portraits and other family treasures.

'Not too much about the poet, now, Bookie. Other people find *others* in this family interesting.'

I have forgotten how many parties were conducted through the house, but the fête raised four hundred pounds altogether—from the horseshoe-throwing, the fancy-work stall, the baking stall, and the rest. Henceforth the Ottregians were much better known to me and I to them, and to walk into the town became a different thing.

Uncle Arthur Mackarness, aged eighty-three, brother to 'Aunt

Tim', was also a visitor at that time, a grand old man of the world. All of us were devoted to the memory of 'Tim', who had died the previous winter, and she was, as she always had been between people, a fine and charming bond among us.

What we all remembered particularly was her wit, which came out of that mild and elegant presence with surprising force and acerbity. Was timidity perhaps induced by relentless clarity of mind in a gentle soul? Anyhow, she was a very real person to all of us. In 1949 I dedicated the *Philosophical Lectures* to her, *in memoriam*, as Miss Daisy Mackarness and to the late Reverend G.H.B.Coleridge. Lord Coleridge teased me about the 'mistake' in my dedication, her real names being Katherine Alethea Marguerite, but she had signed her letters 'Daisy', and old Uncle Arthur was later to come to my defence, writing from Ottery:

' . . . I suppose I must accept your view about my having the book and of course it is especially nice to feel that I have got what would have been my dear sister's copy. All her life she was called 'Daisy' and only quite lately her nickname of 'Tim' crept in, amongst the young members of this family—personally I like to see her name as Daisy in your book—she was so far more widely known by that name than by any other. . . . It is good to hear how much you like this place. I always feel perfectly happy and *so* peaceful here . . .'

In 1946 the Coleridges had been through six lonely war years. in their guest book, since my previous prewar visit, but two names had been entered. The sons were all married and away, and differences in opinions not fully understood between the generations had made the elders feel old, 'old hat' in fact.

The first night at dinner when I inquired about the three sons, Richard, the eldest, was proudly reported on, and James, the youngest. When I asked about John, the middle one, a grim silence. Eyes went down. Finally, with an effort of brave self-command Jessie Coleridge said quietly, 'You didn't know, of course, Bookie, but he was a Conchie.'

'I should think it one of the bravest things for a man to be,' I said at once, simply thinking aloud. Geoffrey gave me a quick look in which relief was visible.

'Not everyone thought in that way in those days,' she said, and he added,

'He went to prison—you know that?—and I must say he did a very tough kind of service, agricultural labourer, and all that. The boy worked jolly hard. And so he should, of course.'

No doubt there had been bitterness and anger, but by now the bafflement, though not altogether gone, had mellowed into something close to respect. John and his wife were going to do even harder work with disturbed children.

In some way I was encouraged to be an adopted daughter in the house, a prodigal returned home, for whom petrol was rashly expended to show the Home Guard defences on the beaches, or even just to make indulgent picnic expeditions. There was the usual teasing and laughter and little jokes—a sweet comfortable time.

As luck would have it, one day, with rain threatening to ruin the hay, I helped the only two available men to take it in, something I couldn't have enjoyed more, but for which I got over-high marks from 'Himself'. It was hot when he fetched me and as we went into the lovely cool of the house for lunch he made the comical but somehow touching announcement: 'Bookie has been working hard. There's to be no teasing her about it either.' As he was the only conceivable teaser at this point, his admonition to old Uncle Arthur and his Old Trout was just his shy way of conveying appreciation.

One of the intimate times was the bath hour. The boiler could be heated only three times a week, fuel being in very short supply, so we all bathed on those days. It must be explained that the plumbing having been introduced long after the original house was built, there was a very odd bathroom, one room divided in two by a partition, wooden below and heavy rippled glass above. This did not go up quite all the way to the ceiling; decently obscured, one could comfortably carry on conversation from tub to tub. The great tri-weekly question was, would I have my bath before dinner with him, or at bedtime with her? I prefer one before dinner but out of politeness chose her time, until I found he was just a little miffed at first, so I varied my bathing hours. Confidences in the warm relaxed conditions of the tubs were easy and unusually frank. The visit to Ottery, as I say, was particularly genial and happy. It was recognized that, now having the photographs, I had no immediate need of using the library (though naturally I did make use of it) and that the visit was a purely affectionate one.

On my departure Geoffrey Coleridge as always took me to the station. The train (luck again) was late. As we paced up and down the station platform he suddenly asked, but thoughtfully as if it were no sudden impulse,

'What would happen, Bookie, to the STC stuff if it were one day all put in store?'

'Deteriorate, like mad,' I said. 'The notebooks would probably go mouldy and in no time be illegible, the annotations on the books perhaps less quickly. Why do you ask?'

'I don't know what's going to happen to the place,' he said, morosely. 'I don't know whether any of the boys will be interested in living here. I find I don't understand the new generation.' I had a very few minutes to take this in, but fortunately there was no sign of the train and there was a pause in which to think wild thoughts.

'Does it mean,' I said, in some trepidation, 'does it mean you would not mind listening to an offer for the whole STC collection, if it were to go to one of the great national libraries like the British Museum or the Bodleian?'

'I should certainly listen to such an offer,' he said, 'but you'll never get anybody to bite, Bookie. Everybody *says* how very valuable these things are, but nobody ever makes me an offer for them. Now people do make me offers for beef cattle. There's something for you with *real* value. Give me bullocks every time! Ah—you and your old poet!' And he gave me a quick hug. 'But remember, if there comes an offer, I shall answer *yes* or *no*. There will be *no* haggling.' There was plenty of food for thought during the train journey up to London. Where should I go for advice?

I went down to Oxford and talked with Miss Seaton, who suggested that Professor Ifor Evans had the sort of worldly wisdom I needed. He and I had corresponded about biographical materials in the notebooks. On August 16, over his good sherry, he discussed my whole question, and with enthusiasm suggested my applying to the Pilgrim Trust. An American philanthropic foundation for the maintenance of things of cultural value in England, it seemed precisely appropriate. The twenty-second of August was the day the secretary of the Pilgrim Trust, Colonel Browne then, later Lord Kilmaine, appointed to see me.

Miserable with a stiff neck, and wrapped up in an old warm tweed suit and a thick scarf, I must have looked a pitiful blue-stocking as I walked across his elegant office, for his first remark was, 'I think I should say at once, Miss Coburn, that we do not make grants to individuals for research.' I was able to assure him that I was out for something much bigger than that, and referred to the Ottery collection.

'Are we talking of fifty pounds or a thousand pounds?' he said at once.

'I don't know,' I said, taking a deep breath, 'but I suspect a good many thousands of pounds.' He cheered up conspicuously.

'Then I'm interested. Go ahead with your story. Tell me all about it.'

I described the collection, and something of the circumstances. He was telling me it was just the very sort of thing that interested them, that they had just bought Isaac Newton's house and library, the John Locke papers, and a big music library for the British Museum, when the telephone rang.

By a motion of his hand he invited me to listen to his end of the conversation.

'You see?' he said, as he hung up. 'You're quite in order. Nay, opportune.' His telephone talk had been all about investments, how difficult to find any; in short, what to do with money! Could I be hearing straight? He went on, however, to say he would proceed slowly. A committee please, five or six persons perhaps, the better-known publicly the better, but they must be knowledgeable about the value of these papers too, a report on the extent and importance of the collection, and a specific valuation. Only then could he take a proposal to his board.

I knew something of what Edmund Blunden had done for the Keats–Shelley memorial library in Rome and although I did not know him personally I wrote to him asking if I could see him. On the 13th of September we had a conversation memorable to me. It took place in one of the barren rooms in *The Times* offices— temporary walls (post-blitz), one big table, two straight chairs, one dry inkwell and an empty umbrella stand. Not exactly cosy. I had been told that Blunden was impossibly diffident, at any rate close-mouthed. He may have been, and I am sure could be, but, like many reserved persons, given a favourite subject, he *poured* out. Mostly about S.T.Coleridge and little about the practical exigency before us. He was rather pessimistic about that—the Shelley memorial in Rome had been a slow and laborious business—but he agreed to try to get a committee. The names he suggested I have forgotten. But the Coleridges—why the difficulties about getting down there? He was interested in the family.

Coleridge was a deeply religious man, he said, and must be dealt with by those who understood this side of him. E.K.Chambers's biography was beneath criticism, too many moral judgements, 'full of the ringing contempt of the self-righteous civil servant. What does he mean by saying S.T.Coleridge was lazy? He just doesn't know what STC's kind of work means! And De Sclincourt! Why do people have to like Wordsworth and hate Coleridge and *vice versa*? Why do people hate what is different from themselves? This is the cause of wars!' He was almost quoting Coleridge's question, 'Why is difference linked with hatred?' Hanson's biography Blunden thought limited, not ripe in knowledge. 'Underestimates the Christ's Hospital influence. Not the man for Coleridge somehow, but of course far better than Chambers.' I came away with an impression of a gentle man bruised, fiery in his attachment to literature, restricted perhaps in his sympathies and tastes, older generation (first war) in his opinions, but for the immediate purpose a man with useful connexions and the right kind of passion. Yes, he would collect our committee, and we would write back and forth, and I would come back next summer and we would try to get the report into the hands of the Pilgrim Trust. Was he practical, I wondered? Yet he was in England, and I perforce had to be in Canada.

The next thing I knew—several months later—he was in Japan, as cultural liaison officer to the British Mission there. No committee had been set up.

One other interview of that summer of '46 startled me. I went to see the Director of the British Museum because the Pilgrim Trust's Colonel Browne had said I should find out at once if the British Museum would be prepared to accept such a gift as the Coleridge Collection, and if not, if the Bodleian would. Sir John Forsdyke was slightly amused. Why is it so many elderly Englishmen take up this relaxed defence—or is it that, being English, and elderly, they can really afford to be amused without bothering to conceal it? Most of the time he talked about Christ's Hospital, Coleridge's school, his own school; he was a Blue Coat boy, too.

'Charles Lamb's idiotic prostration before Coleridge can be understood only in relation to the school. Coleridge was a Grecian —a bright boy—appointed by the Head or the Governors as a sort of senior student-don-in-charge. There were no masters living in— only old women, housekeepers, of a different class entirely—Grecians were looked up to. Lamb never was more than a Deputy-Grecian. Probably because of his stutter for one thing. But he always adored Coleridge as his Grecian.

'Of course we shall accept the Coleridge manuscripts if you give them to us. We'll have to. Why don't you take them off with you to America—sorry, Canada? I believe in scattering these things. Why should they all be here in the Museum? Why don't you take them with you?' All very silly, I thought, disloyal to English scholars, and unrealistic about research, with no concept whatever of the close relation of these manuscripts to the rich collection already in the British Museum. I found him negative—unimaginative—but he had given me an interesting chat about Coleridge's great school.

There was an evening with another member of the Coleridge family that summer, Geoffrey's sister, Phillis Coleridge, and much more interested in her great, great, great uncle the poet. She was a lively character with more ardour and nervous excitability than sober judgment, but no fool either, a woman deeply wounded by life who found solace in an intense High Anglican faith. She suffered endless miseries as the unmarried daughter living with an aged and demanding invalid mother, and yet endeared herself by her unquenched gaiety and capacity for getting things wrong. She was very proud to be a Coleridge, and she knew that 'old STC' was appreciative of women. 'He knew we have a *few* brains, my dear, though of course I haven't any compared with you, dear Kathleen, but don't tell Geoff I said so.' I could talk with her about the whole family.

'But I say, Kathleen, didn't old STC behave rather badly towards Dorothy Wordsworth? Just between ourselves, now?' I was baffled.

'Well, they *were* in love, weren't they? Why didn't he marry her?'

Then I remembered one of the most inaccurate and insensitive books ever to appear on the subject, *Dorothy and William* I think it was called, which propounded just such a theory. So I protested that when Coleridge met Dorothy Wordsworth he was already married to Sarah Fricker. What did she think he should have done, even if it were so? But if Dorothy was ever attracted in that way to him, it was not reciprocal. True, poor 'old STC' soon found he had mis-married and got the wrong Sarah, but that was another story.

'Oh, my dear! What an awful thing—a mistake like that! I say, I do hope you'll clear it all up one day in your book.'

Poor dear 'Auntie Phil' had bought herself a little dream house in 1940 in Knightsbridge and was hardly settled in it before the bombs began. She and her mother moved with nurses and maid to Oxford, where the old lady died at ninety-five. Phil was worn out and an old lady herself by the time she finally settled into her house for her last three years. But that summer of '46 she was back in it, with all her treasures, windows recently repaired after the blitzes, when I wrote and announced myself. I had a *long* letter by return of post, inviting me to Sunday tea at four, and giving explicit and detailed instructions as to how to get there—a perfectly simple Knightsbridge address, but dear Phil, with no sense of direction herself, had never mastered the London underground and always expected guests to lose themselves. There was no time to answer but by telephone. Her voice was high and especially over the telephone she spoke breathlessly at great speed without giving herself time to listen to any reply.

'Hello—Are you there? Is that Kathleen? What? Oh my dear! I say, welcome home and all that. It *is* good to have you back in England. I'm *so* looking forward to seeing you. Sorry I wasn't in when you first called. What? No, I was at Hampton Court for the day, seeing Lady Fisher. So sorry to have missed you. But you will come to tea, won't you? Will you find your way, do you think? Nobody ever does, my dear! What? Well that's simply splendid, Kathleen dear. Then we'll catch up on everything tomorrow, *Sunday*.'

I found Fairholt Street easily enough, with its good eighteenth-century cottages, Auntie Phil's perfectly distinguishable by her

Della Robbia cherub over the door. She admitted me herself, looking a little heavier, and not so worn as when her mother was alive. 'Oh, my dear.' Kiss on right cheek. 'It *is* good to see you, my dear.' Kiss on left cheek. 'Why, you look *wonderful*, my dear Kathleen, do come and sit down for a minute—and then you must come and see my little house.'

The first impression was of low-ceilinged cottage rooms, very dark, and the darker for the fact that there was nowhere two square inches of bare wall, the walls being heavy with huge family portraits, water-colours, miniatures, paintings that once belonged to Aunt Tim, photographs of everybody, prints of paintings of and by ancestors, by the score. When the wall-space gave out, including all the hallway and staircase, screens were found; they blocked up the entrances to the little rooms (or kept out draughts, as you will) so that you watched your step as you sidled in and out. On them hung yet more water-colours and miniatures. The mantels were loaded with miscellaneous objects, and there was an assortment of little tables, footstools and firescreens worked by various somebodies, and fans, some of them framed, some in cases, and corner cabinets full of what looked like dolls' dishes. The house could not possibly have accommodated a cat or a canary. She loved all these things, and amid shouts of laughter told me how a former maid objected to them all and had said it was dangerous during air raids to have 'all that glass about' on the walls; she had wanted Auntie Phil to give them all away, to salvage.

'I said to her, my dear Dorothy, would you have me give my dear father and my grandfather, the Lord Chief Justice there, away to salvage? And she said, "Yes, I should. What are they good for anyhow, Miss? And they're most dangerous." I just told her if a bomb fell on that house we should never know it anyhow, and she might better get used to that idea. You know, my dear, I *have* been glad of having a bit of a sense of humour, and really, to come down at night and see Dorothy sitting in my front room in her tin hat, with her *enormous* feet up on a pouff, it did look *too* killing! But you know, I *was* here alone night after night while Dorothy was out fire-watching and it was a bit frightening. Just a bit.'

She didn't stop long to reflect on that.

'You know, I had a very funny conversation once with the fire warden in this street. I said to him it was silly Dorothy being out, because if a fire ever began here I shouldn't be able to *move* the stirrup pump by myself. It takes two people at least. And he said, "Miss Coleridge, I don't like to have to talk to you about your age, but how old are you?" I said, I don't mind about my age at all. It's nothing whatever to mind about. I'm fifty-nine. (I *was* then fifty-nine). And he said, "Oh, that's all right." And I said, what's *all right*? From what point of view is fifty-nine *all right*?'

Shouts of laughter from her.

'And he said, "Then I don't have to put you down as *aged*. If you were sixty, now, it would have to be *aged*, but not at fifty-nine, miss." So I said, never mind, I shall know that next year I can be considered *aged*, and what's the difference in being considered *aged*? "You have to have special treatment then, miss." "But I should *love* special treatment." I said. "Does it mean they bring a bath chair to your door and wheel you away if there's an accident? I should hop into it with the greatest of pleasure. Don't bother, warden, consider me aged if you like. I shall be, next year!"'

She missed Aunt Tim badly, and told me about her death and the trials of the last years, and brought Tim's tea-set out in my honour because she knew I would recognize it. All this talk about Tim's death a few weeks previously made me a little hesitant about suggesting anything so frivolous as a theatre, but one theatre per visit had been routine with Auntie Phil and me, and I soon discovered she had three suggestions ready to hand. We went to *The First Gentleman*, a play about George IV. It was not necessary for me to brush up my English domestic history, for Phil was keen on royalty. As we waited for the curtain to go up she rambled on.

'Oh, my dear. I say, there must be great times when you and my brother Geoff get together. Are there?'

'Why?'

'Because you're so much alike, my dear, aren't you?'

That was a bit of a blow, so I said, 'You mean we're rather blunt and saucy?'

'Yes, *rather*, a *bit*—it must be fun when you both get going.' She chuckled, relishing the idea—so I admitted to small sessions of speaking out sometimes.

'I'll warrant you do. Wish I could be there to hear it. And I say, my dear, it must be comic to hear you having to defend the old poet to him. He doesn't like poor old STC, does he? Thinks he's rather a blot on the family escutcheon, I think. Besides, doesn't know anything about him ... I say, do you see who's sitting in the Royal Box? Is that Princess Marie Louise? She must be one of the few remaining grandchildren of Queen Victoria—I say, it's jolly sporting of her to come to this play—pretty rough on them, don't you think, having that old reprobate of an uncle?'

I had a reason to be interested in these royal persons, for their existence was linked in an extraordinary way with my Georgian Bay summer life. The nearest town and source of supplies there is Parry Sound. Years ago, when the land on which the town was built was ceded or sold to the municipality, the owner, William Beatty, wished to insert a clause in the deed to prohibit forever the sale of alcoholic liquors on the property. 'Forever' being impossible legally, the clause had to have reference to the lifetime of some person. Beatty chose the last surviving grandchild of his Queen, Victoria. Thus for many decades no whisky was sold in Parry Sound and the inhabitants observed with interest the royal family dropping off one by one; but fate played a trick on Mr Beatty. The Island View Hotel eventually being sold for taxes, all such restrictions against that property were automatically invalid, and Parry Sound did not have to wait for royalty to die.

'Let's see, George IVth must have been her great-great-uncle, wasn't he? I wonder what they are thinking of it? I say, wouldn't it be rum to be royalty? I think they're awfully brave, don't you? Our King has been marvellous during the war ...' I wouldn't be without the memory of that evening for a large legacy.

London was full of Europeans who had managed to spend the war years there instead of in concentration camps, and life for me was greatly deepened because of them. It is tempting to describe them, their problems, their universal admiration for Londoners during the war, and their own courage and wonderful sense of humour in all the circumstances—the Isepps, for instance. Later, Sebastian Isepp restored paintings in the National Gallery, Helli taught singing, and Martin, a youngster hungry for chocolate, was already playing the piano with amazing control. And Emmy Heim, warm, sensitive, elegant as ever, who before the war had taught Toronto to enjoy German *Lieder*, there she was, freezing in several layers of wool under a siren-suit, eager for news of her Canadian friends, and longing for Canada. They made me realize vividly how almost painfully fortunate I had been to have been able to carry on my Coleridge work with the skies all over the world falling. One *knew* it, naturally, with all the imagination permitted of knowledge of what was happening half a world away; but here it was, in the flesh, in survivors, at the dinner table.

Returning home in September I found Toronto especially pleasant, warm and sunny after that grey, cold summer; I felt the richness of it, a Canada lush with melons and peaches and grapes, trees all gold and copper, like the wheat, in the September sun.

In October 1946 there came a first visit from George Whalley. He was teaching in Bishop's University in Lennoxville, Quebec, fresh out of the Canadian Navy (when not on loan to the British Navy). He had had a distinguished career, but of this I knew nothing at the time. I noticed that he sat very upright on a straight chair in my office to discuss Coleridge, Lowes's *Road to Xanadu* and the 'ways of the imagination', 'facts of mind' as Coleridge called them. I do not know who sent him to me. He seemed to have spent many hours on the bridges of destroyers thinking about poems, and the poets that made them, and somehow, he said, 'the compass needle kept coming back to Coleridge'. Either on this first visit or on a second one, but at some early point, we had long discussions about where he should do further post graduate work on his D.V.A. allowance. I suggested he should go to the University of London, only to find that the head of the Toronto Graduate English department, A.S.P. Woodhouse, was making difficulties if Whalley did not decide on Toronto. Nevertheless it was crystal clear that a young man of his stature and training—he already had degrees in classics and theology and had been a Rhodes Scholar at Oxford for three years—ought to go to a university that would allow him to complete his PhD in two years with none of the Toronto nonsense of that day about unnecessary post-graduate lectures and papers. In London he would be close to the British Museum. I also had some reason to fear that the anti-feminism of the head of the department would not make life any easier for my students than for me. While Woodhouse brought pressure to bear on several of the best of them to stay and take a Toronto degree, they nevertheless went, with my blessing, elsewhere—a lamented state of affairs, but necessary to recognize. It was, however, in ways foreseen and unforeseen, for the best, in each case.

In the course of our many hours of talk on these visits I found that George and I had in common an interest in Coleridge's mind—as distinct from his magic—and in what he did analytically and creatively with his reading. I had a post-graduate class working on a survey of Coleridge's reading, but could see that it would not produce any adequate composite result. George took over the whole scheme for his London PhD, and transformed it, thus becoming inevitably the editor of the *Marginalia*. But the story here has overleaped itself.

George was searching for the less formal materials behind the poems and the prose works, and I think it was in the first few moments of conversation, looking very intense, he asked if I knew the whereabouts of the Coleridge notebooks. 'I have been thinking I should like to edit them,' he said unguardedly. Here was a young man who had been risking his life on the high seas while I had been happily reading and transcribing those notebooks that had been his mental escape from the dangers and tedium of war. There was nothing for it but to be as direct and open as he had been.

'If you will pull out the middle drawer of that filing cabinet on your left,' I had to say, 'you will find transcripts of about half of them.' There was the slightest quiver of an eyelid, not enough to prevent him saying at once, 'Well, then, is there anything I can do to help?' He has been helping ever since, with the notebooks and hundreds of chores large and small, in an unselfregarding way that has to be experienced to be imagined. His high standards of civility and concern for the deepest and highest ends of research have affected the whole Coleridge enterprise.

In 1947 my own work concentrated mainly on the *Philosophical Lectures*, to complete them according to contract. But from time to time a question nagged. What about the committee to report to the Pilgrim Trust on the Ottery collection? There had been no word from Blunden.

V

1947–1951

The manuscript of the *Philosophical Lectures* went off in November 1947 to the Pilot Press. That was a very bad winter in England, cold, with floods, and long and numerous power cuts. A struggling new publishing house could not cope with the unforeseen printing problems and thus my manuscript went through a chain of vicissitudes. After having been marked up for an English typesetter it was flown to the Pilot Press, New York; then to Pellegrini & Cudahy, where it was marked again in a totally different American style; then suddenly I received a cable to send it at once back to London; changes in British fiscal regulations would have made it impossible, as I understood it, for Pilot Press London to import its own sheets from the United States. The printer's copy, by now having gone through so many countermanded markings, was barely intelligible; how any English printer finally produced anything remotely corresponding to Coleridge's intentions and mine is beyond guessing. Error and inconsistency and misunderstanding were hideously compounded in the galleys. Proof-reading in England was for me a nightmare, and so must have been the bill for corrections which Pilot Press in fairness took on itself.

In August 1948 after the proofs were read, as a much-needed stretching exercise after close confinement, I repeated with Barbara Rooke the Wordsworth-Coleridge Scottish Tour of August 1803. No jaunting car for us, only bicycles. Nor did our difficulties arise over the three beds that Wordsworth and Dorothy and Coleridge worried about; it was ration cards we had to contend with. The further north we went the less grim the encounter when we presented them, but in the lowlands we were shocked sometimes to be refused our ration of eggs and meat. Coleridge's descriptions in his notebooks, in very faint pencil, of his days in Scotland, were a little more legible on the spot, for we had taken some photographed pages along. Moreover, in following the actual trail our appreciation of his energy, his strenuousness, grew. He was an indefatigible climber, always one for up and over, the high road rather than the low, an impression later re-confirmed in Sicily and Italy. Another result of reading some of the Scottish tour memoranda on the terrain was understanding how some of the glosses on *The Ancient Mariner* probably originated there, in a 'breeze of feeling' similar to the feelings of 1797 in Wordsworth's company in another lonely landscape, the wild stretches of the northwest Devon coast where *The Rime of the Ancient Mariner* was conceived. In 1803 in Scotland he was jotting down entries referring to ships' sails, spirits, phantoms, loneliness and homelessness, like these:

'Shadows over Corn and Woods like the motion of the Air in Sails'

' ... The Raindrops on the Lake [compared] to an army of spirits, or Faeries, on a wilderness of White Sand/Multitude & Joyance, motion or a moving'

'The White mists ... giving phantoms of motion even to the Hills'

'Young trees in the valley below ... seemed as if they had ... no abiding place'

In a 'loneliness and fixedness' similar to the Mariner's he wrote,

' ... I have no dear Heart that loves my Verses ...'

In 1817, when he was adding those moving glosses in the margins of *The Ancient Mariner*, did associations take him back not only to 1797, when the poem was written, but to 1803, when he was identifying himself more and more with his own ancient mariner?

Our arduous bicycle tour, fact-finding rather than sentimental, gave one a sense of physical realities, felt on the skin and through the eyes, and also in intangible ways it brought many insights together; at the very least such direct experience protects one against some kinds of ignorant error.

Under pressure on all sides the Pilot Press was desperately trying to honour its contract and produce the *Philosophical Lectures*. Perhaps the *Philosophical Lectures* helped to sink the Pilot Press; almost certainly that book was the final straw on the camel's back.

The index had been overlooked in their estimates of our time-schedule, but I could not agree to publishing it without one, so I was given three days (and nights) in which to produce it. I should know better now. Perhaps it is better than no index, I am not sure. People have used it. I have myself used it, finding it almost intolerable. In justice I should add that the printer, after doing most exemplary difficult work on the text, when he came to the index seems in his haste to have scrambled the type on the floor; some index entries make utter nonsense. However, the book came out (after a long delay in the bindery) in May 1949. The Pilot Press had gone bankrupt. The best moment was a postcard, the morning after publication day, from that terror of Oxford Common Rooms and committees, Humphry House. He was kind and complimentary, knowing no doubt from his own sensibility what fears the day can bring, especially for a first book. Actually his card alarmed me, for, until it came, I was entirely without the consciousness that anyone would ever see the book or read it, let alone anyone as fiercely critical as Humphry House. That it would have an audience, and I an exposure, had never occurred to me; the full realization of having planted a book that now appeared full grown in covers and jacket before the eyes of the public came as a great shock. It was just another piece of my good fortune not to have energy-destroying worries. At this time, in England for a year on an International Federation of University Women's Travelling Fellowship, I was more concerned about the Ottery collection, and about puzzling out notebook entries, than I was about the fate of the printed and published *Philosophical Lectures*.

Lowes had died in 1945, and Harvard could not track down his trunkful of notes. I had hoped to use them, with his initials at the appropriate places. As I knew from him of Helen Waddell's interest in his projected edition of the one notebook in the British Museum, I wrote to her. The reply was charming, as one would have expected, but not useful:

32 Primrose Hill Road,
N.W.3.
February 6 1949

'... I think I urged on my publishers and on himself [Lowes] the facsimile text of the Gutch Memorandum Book, which he used in *The Road to Xanadu*. And I believe I still have a facsimile of it. The BM allowed Constable's to have it photographed. I imagine he and I talked over and round and through it—I remember it as the most exciting bran tub dip. And he used to say it was I and not he who should edit it—but that was quite fantastic. He may have said it in Harvard, for now and then I hear of it: but there was no solid foundation. The twelfth, not the late eighteenth, was my century: but acting, as I did then, as adviser to Constable, I sometimes had to range. And the memory of that notebook still goes to my head …

It is a tragedy that no one seems to know where the Livingston Lowes' MSS are. Some one wrote to me from—I think Toronto years ago, in the hope that I might know: for I gather that Harvard can find nothing …'

Mea culpa. I was the Toronto inquirer. But she was much shaken by the 1944 bombardment, to which she had referred in the first part of the letter, and by this time she was often ill. Alas, one of those persons one would wish to have known.

As to recommendations to the Pilgrim Trust on the Ottery Collection, the whole affair was in suspension. I saw Colonel Browne (now Lord Kilmaine) again. Yes, the Pilgrim Trust would be interested. Edmund Blunden was still uncommunicative in Japan. No committee had been formed. Miss Seaton suggested I should go to Professor Basil Willey for advice. A Cambridge woman herself, her thoughts easily travelled there. So I went to Cambridge and had the first of many happy encounters with him.

He took me out to lunch and was, I think, more than a little surprised at my story. He first raised the practical donnish question whether it was in my interest to put the things in the British Museum—if they were not better at Ottery till I had finished with them, perhaps a shrewd attempt to sound me. I said, I am sure with comic solemnity, that I thought the matter too important—more important than the editing; we had a chance to acquire these manuscripts for posterity; the library might otherwise be sold at auction and dispersed, and what a tragedy for scholars, especially English scholars, that would be! Why should I not be ready to take any personal chances involved? We talked about a committee. He had already invited Humphry House to meet us after lunch. I did not know him, and perhaps would not have invited him to join the committee if I had, but he became a tower of strength. E.M.W. Tillyard was suggested, as Master of Coleridge's old college, Jesus; Harold Nicolson; and of course, Edmund Blunden. They all accepted their rôles, but so far as I remember, Tillyard and Nicolson did not attend any meetings of the committee.

We had to do two things: write a persuasive recommendation to the Pilgrim Trust and try to get the collection valued. When the committee met, Basil Willey offered to write to somebody in Quaritch's who, he thought, would do the valuation personally and unofficially, or at least would know how we should go about it. Harold Nicolson had agreed to see me and to have the thing explained. I confess I went to him very much in hope of seeing Vita Sackville-West, she of the wonderful voice reading *The Land* and the friend of Virginia Woolf, but there was plenty of excitement without all that. I went armed with some photographs to show to Harold Nicolson. He looked that day rather red and beef-eaterish and very much the diplomatic man of the world—but by the end of tea he warmed up about Coleridge, envied me the photographs, and agreed to help. He belonged to the same London club, he said, with Harold Macmillan, Chairman of the Pilgrim Trust, and Lord Kilmaine. Anyway, he would do what he could. If he knew 'a really bright young man looking for a literary subject' he thought the best subject he could suggest and would suggest would be Coleridge—but 'he would have to be a *very* bright young man.' I left feeling slightly irritated at not being a bright young man, and not being quite bright enough to know exactly what he was trying to say to me. Maybe he was being rude to me, but I didn't feel sure enough of that to be angry, and why be angry? Maybe he didn't realize quite how involved I was. After all, he was an outsider in Coleridge matters, helpful though he might be. Anyway, I couldn't go back on my tracks, and I wasn't going to be unduly disturbed by a passing remark, whether it had more in it than met the eye or not. I decided to play the diplomat too, even with my own feelings.

Basil Willey's letter—to the friend in Quaritch's—misfired. The friend was just retiring, or retired, and somehow this highly confidential letter was accidentally turned over to the firm. Our committee met again in Cambridge in some distress. Quaritch wanted to go down straight away to Ottery to see the collection. They

would charge something like a hundred guineas for valuing, plus
one percent of the value plus expenses. As we had no money,
where could the valuation fee come from? Having carefully not dis-
closed any information all this time to any bookseller whatever, or
anybody else, for that matter, I was alarmed. The committee agreed
that Quaritch had to be held off, firmly but discreetly, for here
could be a threat to disperse the collection, the very thing we were
trying to avoid. As the most innocent-looking of our number, I was
nominated to go to see them. I made an appointment for a certain
afternoon, hour indefinite, at Quaritch's. Purposely, and because I
did not wish to waste good British Museum time, I arrived about
ten minutes before the five o'clock closing time. Never before, or
since, have I felt the announcement of my name produce such an
electric current. Quickly I was passed on to a second rather more
important clerk, and was led over to a bookcase where he pushed a
button, and *presto!* the bookcase opened into another carpeted
room lined with books. We walked across it—to another button,
and another bookcase opened on to even richer carpet and more
lavishly-bound books, and more sumptuous furnishings. From
behind a desk a long-legged individual rose and with what I regarded as a sinister smile (partly from ill-fitting dentures) said,
'How do you do, Miss Coburn. I must first of all offer you my
congratulations on having so nearly completed your great work.'
This took me aback and gave me furiously to think for a second or
two while I was supposed to be flustered with modesty or shyness.
The committee had had some discussion as to whether publication
of the notebooks would diminish the value of the originals. We
did not know, but we though that *if it did* affect the value at all, it
would, for a time anyhow, affect the price adversely. Now this un-
founded too shiny compliment told me at once that the question
was of considerable interest to a bookseller.

So I replied truthfully that publication was far off yet—would
take years probably. The committee had agreed that I should be
vague about Quaritch's correspondence with us, find out what they
proposed, and let them know as little as possible. I discovered they
already knew I was going down to Ottery, and wanted to send someone down while I was there. We feared that they might persuade
Lord Coleridge to take some course more advantageous to them
than to scholarship, such as selling the collection bit by bit. I

was not altogether afraid of that, Geoffrey Coleridge having made it clear that he would feel justified in selling the collection only if it went to one of the great national libraries, but one never knows what can happen. My concerns were that the collection should be preserved intact, and that the whole transaction should be securely carried out with the least possible irritation and worry to the Coleridges; if it caused too much conflict and disturbance of his peace, Lord Coleridge might easily call off the whole thing.

So I stalled, was uncertain of my Ottery dates, thanked them for their offer to help, and would let them know, or the committee would, whenever we felt the moment had come for them to be of use. I pointed out, as one speaking with authority, that the last thing they should do was to disturb our talks with Lord Coleridge at this stage. I felt in that inner office that I was a fly in a very sticky spider's web, and that a wrong step would cut off a narrow escape. My distrust of all the commercial urgency was perhaps rather more an indication of the fly's innocence than of anything wrong with the spider's instinct for self-preservation. Still, some cause for worry was confirmed when a few days later in Ottery I answered a trunk call from Quaritch's to me in the Chanter's House. Lord Coleridge was out of the house, so at lunch I told him that Quaritch had got wind of our intentions and was beginning to pester. 'I hope you told them to mind their own business,' he said.

We had our plans. There was my old 1931 list, a complete though not very detailed description, of books and manuscripts in the collection. The committee showed it discreetly to two eminent librarians connected with two different institutions, neither of which permitted their staffs to make official valuations. One of them suggested a sum, casually and with all sorts of caveats, the other hinted at three times as much. In the event we were so fortunate as to have help from a young bibliophile especially knowledgeable about sale catalogues, who agreed to take a bicycling holiday in Devonshire and to drop in at Ottery while I was there; David Rogers saved the day for us. He and I went over the old list, item by item, taking the books from the shelves, and discussing the relevance of every piece of manuscript. Off he went, studied his sale catalogues, made his guesses at the contemporary market, and arrived at a sum close to the higher one already mooted. His estimates were checked by the best authorities outside the trade, and the sum of ten thousand pounds was agreed upon, the pound in 1949 being still at par, ($4.98). It now remained to write the report to the Pilgrim Trust.

Humphry took me to lunch at the Swan in Southampton Place and made it clear that he was writing the report and asked me if it could not be sent without my signature, i.e. the implication was that gallant things would be said about my services in the affair that could not be said if I signed it. I realized at the time that this was a poor, perhaps pitiful tack, but I was soon off for home, and hard-pressed in the Museum; I had spent a lot of time already in the business, and convinced myself that my signature didn't matter a hoot. Yet I had the uncomfortable feeling that such a suggestion would never have been made to a man, and that 'traps do lurk'. They did. Some things wholly outside the main transaction went into the report to which I should not have agreed. A part of the collection, manuscripts having to do with members of the family close to Newman, Keble, and the Oxford Movement, went to the Bodleian. With that I agreed. But unknown to me it was arranged that the photographs of the notebooks I had put in the British Museum in 1937 should be turned over to Jesus College, Cambridge. The argument ran that the British Museum, having the originals, would have no need of the photographs. Informed too late, I objected nevertheless, on the grounds that some of the notebooks were fragile, and that for most purposes the photographs would serve in general use, with the manuscripts available when need arose. I am not happy that time has confirmed the force of my unavailing protest. Gratifyingly from one point of view, the notebooks have been in constant use, but as a result, a few readings have disappeared from worn page-corners.

Surely institutions should not give away gifts without consulting the donors, In all the talk that went on between the Museum and some members of the committee, certain things were lost sight of. The moral for me was that I ought to have insisted on seeing that report through to the end.

Early in 1949, Basil Willey wrote to me that the offer for the collection had been made by the Pilgrim Trust and had been accepted in principle. But there were still rocks in the waters ahead. I had from 'Himself' the following letter, among others:

'21.8.49. My dear Bookie,
   Yes, I have had the absurd offer of £10,000 which, in the interests purely of literature, I have generously accepted ...'

He went on about how the law was dragging on, an Order of the Court being required before the sale could be completed and the gift accepted by the BM, winding up in his usual vein,

'I shall be writing to you again but in the meantime I hope you grasp that my main object in accepting provisionally such a trifling sum is to rid myself of peripatetic professors & others of that ilk interested in such a puerile & sterile subject.
Anyhow best love to you ...
                                  Yrs aff:
                                      C'

While the law was 'dragging on' over the Ottery collection going to the British Museum, the summer of 1950 on Georgian Bay was not for a minute dragging for me. It was a summer of continuing the struggle to get the contents of some fifteen of the earlier notebooks in order, and tussling with STC's meanings and intentions. In this sort of work there are the intense pleasures of both involvement and detachment. Coleridge demands concentrated attention. One can be swept off one's balance altogether by the surprises round every corner—on the one hand by his panoramic surview of the whole of human intellectual history—the sciences, for instance, and the marginal between animate and inanimate nature—and on the other by his quick eye for the flower at his feet, the movement of a bird's bill, or the meeting-point of fear and anger. I was impatient with some of his theological preoccupations, but felt I was beginning to grasp his interest in Kant, and his ambivalence about the post-Kantian German metaphysics, and to know that the too rough and too ready dubbing him a German transcendental idealist was wrong. For all his 'abstruse research' he had his feet on English earth. His psychological observations, neither English nor German, became more astonishing the further I read and understood the notebooks.
   In these insights I was greatly helped by Jessie's critical attitude towards all metaphysics whatever, while she was hammering out

G.E.Moore for herself. I perforce had to contend with her admiration for the positivists and to debate what I took to be a misunderstanding of the poetic and philosophic imagination as they come together in Coleridge. His anticipations of Freud brought her part way round, a long way; but positivism seemed to me then, as it does now more and more clearly, the negation of an important dynamic in the human mind, by its own premises more negative than positive. To the last, all our arguments seemed to end in agreeing to the general truth of Goethe's and Coleridge's division of all minds into two camps, Aristotelian and Platonist, and that we were in different ones. She was a refreshing antidote to all idealist idolaters of Coleridge and forced me on to firmer ground. No talk with anyone has ever been a sharper, more critical, more pleasurable stimulus to my work.

The pattern of the days was, as I have said, a good four-hour stint of Coleridge every morning, six days a week, guests or no guests. In bad weather Coleridge got the afternoons too, but mostly the afternoons were active; fishing, wooding expeditions collecting roots for the fireplace, blueberrying, or just canoeing among the bare outer rocks; or a visit to Surprise Bay for its flowers, especially cardinal flower, or to Johnson's Bay for another mood entirely— vast swampy stretches showing deer tracks and places where deer or bear had been lying in the grass. Then the lovely long sociable evenings.

The calm of this routine was somewhat shattered by the arrival of a manuscript from my father—about thirty of his personal anecdotes, very badly typed by his own two-finger method. Would I blue-pencil them for him?

I was appalled, and trapped, for I had urged on him the writing out of all those yarns with which he had rocked the family dinner table for years, and which he had told and retold to friends and strangers alike, tales of little comedies and tragedies he had seen taking place all round him, Irish-fashion. Some of the human episodes he had lived through were significant enough as moments in Canadian social history and had therefore more than a personal interest. In his voice, accompanied by his enthusiastic gestures, his anecdotes were vivid and captured an audience, but in the manuscript he sent me there was no twinkle in the eye; the tone was flat and unrecognizable. The dialogue was as stiff as the two fingers with which he poked the keys. He was no longer an Ancient Mariner buttonholing a Wedding Guest, he was not even a parson in good pulpit form, he was suddenly trying to be an 'author'. But what to say? Here was a man in his seventies, retired, and putting on paper what had entertained him and us for a lifetime. Could he stand an honest criticism or would he be so cruelly dispirited as not to try again? His own openness demanded frankness, so I wrote a brutal 'this will never do' sort of letter, blue-pencilled his manuscript unsparingly, and told him to be himself, with examples. I worried as I returned the manuscript, but I needn't have done. He bounced back like the best of students, full of nothing but gratitude and energy, and rewrote the lot, with increased enthusiasm.

The title was fun. Many of the stories had to do with his battles for justice in some good cause or other. As he was fond in various contexts of quoting Oliver Cromwell, I suggested more mischievously than seriously, *Keep Your Powder Dry*. His publishers in the end altered it to *I Kept My Powder Dry*, and when I pointed out that perhaps the implication was, for a parson, a bit uncanonical ('Other people might trust in God, but I kept my powder dry'), he pooh-poohed me, perfectly sure of his ground. The book gave him immense pleasure, and was followed by another. He delighted in pointing out to me that his sales were better than mine for *The Grandmothers*.

In December of 1949 I had another letter from Geoffrey Coleridge, thanking me for a copy of *The Grandmothers*. He wrote,

'It is well worth the trouble of making out a catalogue card for it and that is a great compliment from *me*! I am about half-way through already, and I am using as a book marker in it 'Bass fishing. Georgian Bay' a postcard addressed to me in your fair hand last August.

You will no doubt be wondering why I do not let you know what is happening about the STC manuscripts & the answer is 'because nothing has happened'. The BM lawyers, & scholars are, I suppose, all hibernating. Last week a young man wanted to come & study Behmen's Works for a thesis for his BLitt & I dealt with him in what I hope was an effective way. His ilk should all join in sticking pins into the BM.

To end on a serious note, it is very sweet of you to send a copy of your book & we appreciate it very much . . .
                                    Yours aff:
                                    Coleridge'

'27.2.50.   My dear Bookie,
    No doubt you know by now that the sale of STC papers has now been concluded subject to the order of the Court? I insisted that the expenses of obtaining the Order (estimated at £200) should be paid by the purchasers who required it, & the price now agreed is £10,200 instead of £10,000 originally offered. Thus ends satisfactorily to all parties these prolonged negotiations which you have been so largely instrumental in initiating & carrying through & from my side of the bargain I thank you! . . . Now of course there will be no further need of invading the Chanter's House . . . Love from us to you . . .
                                    Yrs ever
                                    Coleridge'

The legal processes and the actual exchange of money and manuscripts took some months. Geoffrey Coleridge grew impatient.

'9.7.50.   [Dear Bookie,]
Enclosed please find—& answer—latest piffle from some egregious ass. Have told him I am forwarding to you for answer but meanwhile to stay away from me & leave Note Books alone unless he gets your permission. Please send me a letter from yourself to pass on to other lunatics who write.
Meanwhile the law drags on: I have had Mr Mackarness [Uncle Arthur] here staying for a fortnight & have dug every pin I have into him & I hope the BM will do the same with their lawyer . . .
Love to my Amanuensis [Barbara Rooke] but not so much to you with whom I am getting somewhat fed up . . .'

By May 1951 the Ottery transaction was concluded and the collection was accepted by the British Museum from the Pilgrim Trust. Later Humphry House told me that the British Museum, with some internal dissension, had baulked at the £200 search fee until someone brought pressure to bear. The new Director, however, had urged it. 'Some of them were going to let a £10,000 gift go for not wanting to spend £200 on STC!' Humphry raged.

I was planning to go to England for the 1951 summer and had another characteristic letter from Geoffrey.

'9.5.51.

. . . *Inquiring Spirit* has arrived. I may say that the educated of this country spell the word 'enquire'—but you wouldn't know that. Obviously, on reading the introduction, you have sat down with a dictionary & looked out a lot of long words & strung them together hoping that you have filled in the blanks between them to make sense of the whole. Never mind, it is an imposing volume of learning & I am proud to have it here & thank you *very much*. My great grandson will probably sell it to the BM for £10,000.

After letters from Directors, Principals, Keepers of Manuscripts & Professors together with many another rejoicing in weird titles—no barons—I do think the manuscripts may soon start their travels & be settled in the B.M. before you get to England: I wish you many a happy day *there* enjoying the illegible scribblings of the bard. Anyhow we hope to be away in July so you can't come here *then*! The interest on 'the pile of gold rolling into Ottery' will just about pay for the recent rise in wages here! . . . I am in a hurry for post so bless you my dear & come & see us when you are over & ever so many thanks.

Yrs aff.
C'

On the 28th July 1951, *The Times* carried at the top of the Home News column the following:

NOTEBOOKS OF COLERIDGE
Collection acquired by British Museum

The generosity of the Pilgrim Trust has enabled the British Museum to acquire a fine collection of manuscripts and printed books of Samuel Taylor Coleridge. The manuscripts consist principally of a series of 55 notebooks, ranging in date from 1794 to 1834, thus covering the whole of Coleridge's adult life.

They comprise over 7,000 pages, packed with criticisms,

notes for lectures and articles, quotations, drafts of poems or
prose works, travel notes and memoranda of all kinds, and pre-
serve an almost continuous record of the inner workings of his
varied and powerful intellect, just as the celebrated *Table Talk*
preserves fragments of his brilliant conversation. Though many
extracts from these notebooks have been printed in a succession
of publications, beginning with the *Anima Poetae* of the poet's
grandson, E.H.Coleridge, much valuable material still remains.

Outstanding among other manuscripts is the "Ottery copy-
book", into which Coleridge copied 20 of his earliest poems,
written between 1789 and 1791, for members of his family at
Ottery St Mary. Other volumes include letters from and to
various members of the family, including 21 written by Coleridge
himself.

EXAMPLES OF MARGINALIA

The printed books include nearly 200 volumes from Coleridge's library, and among them are no fewer than 88 works
containing examples of his manuscript annotations— the celebrated marginalia which he himself regarded as almost an
integral part of his literary work. The museum already possessed
exactly 100 printed works with manuscript notes by Coleridge.

But still the transfer to the Museum was not quite complete.

Lady Coleridge's letters at the beginning of that 1951 summer
were numerous. They give part of the picture, and convey the
sweetness of her affectionate, utterly selfless nature, and also her
sense of fun. (She often signed herself as she did here because
after one visit, when they several times referred to themselves as
'aged frumps', I called them the Frumps.)

'May 21st [1951]
Dearest Bookie   This is just a hurried line, hoping to catch
you before you sail . . . come to us in June on any date you like,
but best of all would be if you could come down with the gents
from the BM & help them collect the precious treasures of your
beloved old STC . . . but anyhow you come as you suggest in
the latter half of June when you can best fit us in, or best of all
if you can come hand in hand with the Bookies from the BM
anyhow it will be a joy to see you whenever you come & its sweet

of you to want to visit such a pair of old fogies as you will find here, creaking with age, . . . All our love Bookie dear, till we meet again & the sooner the better.

Yr ever loving Frump'

Then her next one three weeks later told me that

'the removal was done with the greatest rapidity & neatness by that very nice Mr Skeat who seemed to really enjoy his little visit . . .' Then, after more welcoming noises about my proposed visit,
'. . . can't you picture the unholy glee of Himself as he saw them [the manuscripts] depart?!!
Much love—
Your affec
Female Frump'

There had in fact been some confusion as I discovered when I saw T.C.Skeat, and as a result I found when I got to Ottery a few things that had been left behind.

'Of course,' Lord Coleridge said, 'they didn't do it properly. Those white collar fellows. Never do. Pack them up, Bookie. You'll have to do it now. We'll send them to the B.M. *C.O.D.*!'

So I put together the last of the collection into an ancient frumpish suitcase, took it up to London with me in the train, and had the pleasure of delivering it with my own hands to the Department of Manuscripts.

VI

1950–1952

It is necessary to back-track a little.

During much of the bother about getting the Ottery Collection into the British Museum I had been working on the selections from Coleridge's prose that became *Inquiring Spirit* (*pace* Geoffrey Coleridge, it was Samuel Taylor Coleridge's spelling and very deliberately chosen for its emphasis on the *in* prefix, deeply significant to STC). Alongside notebooks work, this was relaxation in the evenings, but the two tasks fed each other.

In earlier conversations with Charles Madge while we were working on the *Philosophical Lectures*, I had suggested it was high time someone prepared an anthology of excerpts from Coleridge's prose to show his relevance to modern thinking. Alas! when I took the manuscript in 1949 in to the Pilot Press, Madge, the enthusiastic Coleridgian, was gone, the offices were empty, and everything was in the disarray and sadness of bankruptcy.

It happened for reasons now forgotten that I was to meet Geoffrey Grigson that day. We did not know each other, but we had a rendezvous on the steps of the British Museum. Hardly had we introduced ourselves before he said,

'So you have been living in Highgate? Have you gone to see the old boy's tomb? Shocking, isn't it? Nobody looks after it. Imagine all those schoolboys seeing it in their schoolyard every day, littered with paper and orange peel that tramps have left—that's the way we treat our poets. There's a large crack in the cement now—you could stick your umbrella in and give the old chap a poke if you wanted to!'

We talked about this and that; he was at the time making a selection from the poems of William Barnes. I found his energy, his real concern for poetry and his rudeness towards academic priggishness refreshing. At some pause in our talk he finally came out with what may have been his main reason for inviting me to lunch.

'Well,' he said, 'your publisher's gone bust! What are you going to do?'

I hadn't the slightest idea, and was so rash as to say so. 'And,' I added, 'I have a manuscript in my bag that they asked for and now cannot take.'

With a wonderful grin, Geoffrey stretched out an acquisitive hand. 'Gimme!' he said.

How did I, who expected to beseech on bended knee, know the hunger of publishers in the nineteen-fifties for manuscripts? Grigson was a reader for Routledge & Kegan Paul, and before long I was in Tom Ragg's office singing a contract for *Inquiring Spirit* in which there was a clause giving Routledge & Kegan Paul first refusal of the Coleridge *Notebooks*. A certain levity was in the air. It was partly induced by Tom Ragg's false teeth; one tried to make him laugh, not only because amusement was natural to him, but also for his fascinating struggle to hold on to those uppers through his mirth. When I questioned the *Notebooks* clause he brushed it off.

'Oh, that's not really serious, Miss Coburn,' said he. 'All you have to do when you're ready to offer the Notebooks to us is to insist on royalties of say 50%!' So light-heartedly did we take a fateful first step.

In the autumn, just as I was about to sail for home, Helen Darbishire urged me to see in Windsor Joanna Hutchinson, great-grand-daughter of Thomas Hutchinson, a brother of Mrs Words-worth. She had, Miss Darbishire promised, 'a good many things' of interest to me. As indeed she might, I reflected, for her great-great-aunt, Sara Hutchinson, Mrs Wordsworth's sister, was Coleridge's one great love. What had she left behind? Yet, pushed for time, I very nearly missed that introduction and all the gaiety it added to life. However, tossing in the manuscript of *Inquiring Spirit* (having completed it that morning at 5 a.m. in Highgate) before any-one was astir in Broadway House, Carter Lane, I caught an early bus for Windsor.

In her fifties, Joanna Hutchinson was taking care of two aged ladies, one out of old friendship, and the other out of gratitude for the shelter of a Windsor roof during the war. During the first London blitz Joanna had kept certain Wordsworth items, and Sara Hutchinson's letters and other family papers, in a suitcase under

her bed, so that if things began to crumble round her she could
seize her invalid mother and the suitcase and run. Best to guard
her letters with her own body. 'Better than putting the manuscripts in a bank where in an emergency one would never know
whether family documents would have any sort of attention.'

Joanna's was a lovely firmly-modelled face, rather narrow than
round, with a good forehead and all the lines bevelled; she had
bright blue eyes and elegant white hair. A passionate Wordsworth-
ian, when Bateson's *Wordsworth* came out suggesting in rather
careless terms that Wordsworth's relation to his sister was unconsciously incestuous, she thought there ought to be a law of *post-
humous* libel to put Bateson behind bars. She was never lovelier
than during an outburst of blunt speaking or indignation, especially
when she could then be made to break into laughter.

She had more than a hundred of Sara Hutchinson's letters, only
a few of which she had been able to read (most of them are much
cross-written and she had not the patience, nor, poor lady, the
time) but what she did read had endeared Sara to her, and therefore, indirectly, Coleridge. She just hoped there would be no
scandal! The first draft transcript was made for me by Anne and
Fernando Renier, through 1950; my own work on the letters was
held up until about 1952–3, the Coleridge notebooks having a
natural priority. After Sara's *Letters* were published in 1954 no one
read through them so often as Joanna, nor with more relish, and no
one will quote from them more aptly.

Joanna and I came to love each other dearly, to 'blow off' to
each other, and dear Joanna even more than I, sometimes, needed a
thoroughly good 'blow'. We had at least one spree every time I was
in England—luncheon and a matinée. 'Anything you like except a
musical, dear Kathleen.' She loved talk, especially about the
Wordsworth circle, she loved the theatre, she was a good asker of
clear-headed questions, and she laughed. One particular explosion,
several summers later, will live with me always. She and her aged
cronies were alarmed at threatened cuts in British railway lines.
'We really are too old to travel in buses, with our luggage and all,'
she said, distressful possibilities in her mind's eye. After all, she
had to look after two others, one nearly blind, both much older
than herself. I had just read an article about some proposed new
hovercraft type of locomotion and told her about it, how it didn't

need railway tracks, or roads, and travelled just a few feet above the ground, over fields and hedges. 'What a marvellous thing, Kathleen dear!' Her blue eyes widened, and were all seriousness.

'Do we get inside them—or do we clap them on our backs?' She was, as usual, the first to shout with laughter at her own absurdity.

1951 was the summer of the Sugar Ray Robinson–Turpin fight, and Sugar Ray's arrival in England with a monkey, a troup of retainers, a large magenta car, and all his beefsteaks, had received a good deal of hostile publicity. In the middle of a serious conversation in a Windsor street (doubtless having to do with poetic events of a hundred and fifty years before) Joanna squealed softly and said, 'Kathleen dear, I am so sorry to interrupt, but do you see that *monstrous* hideous pink automobile over there? Windsor is getting full of the most horrible kinds of tourists!'

'Not only do I see it, I can tell you who owns it!' I said. She was flabbergasted that I should even know about Sugar Ray Robinson. A few days later, in London through my open window on a warm summer evening, I heard the ringside broadcast, coming from the 'local' nearby. The excitement was clearly rising, for there was a good deal of international tension connected with that fight; having no wireless, I went across to listen. When it was over, three triumphant cheers were given for Turpin, treats went round, and the old boy sitting beside me growled, 'Our lad can do on the rations wot 'e could na' do on all them beefsteaks, eh?' Joanna telephoned me to say in shocked astonishment at herself that she had listened to it too!

Be it heaven or hell, if it must be one or other, I hope Joanna will be there. Her sense of humour was truly unfailing, to the very end, which came of a painful cancer in 1966. She had been vociferous against the introduction of decimal coinage, and with her last smile and the last of her voice she said sweetly to Muriel Bridge, her dearest and oldest friend, 'Well, dear, I shan't have to learn the decimals now, shall I?'

That 1951 Festival of Britain summer I also came to know Helen Darbishire better. She had been Principal of Somerville in my time in Oxford, but now I knew her, as we talked our 'shop' several times in Oxford and London, as the toughest-minded of the Wordsworthians I had met; not overlooking Mrs Rawnsley, who gave me tea at Allan Bank, and told very unsentimental anecdotes about Wordsworth as she escorted me to Dove Cottage and locked up after me each day.

The first sallies into Dove Cottage in 1933 had been very restricted. What exactly did I wish to see there? Not knowing in the absence of a printed catalogue exactly what was there, it was hard to answer. There was an impression among the very few Coleridgians of that day that we were somehow suspect in Grasmere—from a rival camp. Certainly the Trustees were feeling their way in the administration of their Wordsworth collection. There seemed to linger some of the old conflict between Wordsworth and STC that was unresolved in life. But having tested the ice, the custodians soon broke it when they felt sure one had sympathy and was not plotting against Wordsworth's reputation. In those early days before an old smithy became the library, one worked in the little upper room in Dove Cottage itself, while Emily Kirkbride, guide and caretaker from across the road, showed a perpetual stream of visitors through the house. A great character, she sometimes added a touch of her own invention to her tales of Wordsworth's suitcase and Dorothy's housekeeping, but she had the right attitude to her private laureate all the same. And when her tours were over and the light of day gone (there was no other), she made tea for the two of us where Coleridge and the Wordsworths had had it, where they had dried their wet clothes after walks, where his letters to them were read aloud, where he read parts of *Christabel* to them.

Expeditions to the Lakes, especially to the Wordsworth collection in Grasmere, and to Keswick, were essential to understanding my problems and delightful in many different ways. In a long project like the Coleridge Notebooks it is not sufficient to go once and look through some pertinent collection of unknown materials. What will shriek out its relevance in relation to one stage of the work, one period of time, one subject of interest, may easily be passed over, its significance unrealized, at another time. I have gone to Grasmere at least once in connexion with each of the five volumes, sometimes twice.

But the rewards were not by any means all among the manuscripts, for it would have been physically impossible to resist a walk to Easedale Tarn, a glimpse of Wastdale, a climb up Helvellyn, not just sentimental journeys, also thoroughly good walks. I began to love the Lake District once I had accepted it as a walker's country, not for a Canadian canoe. Like all landscapes, it must be enjoyed for itself and its own qualities, not by comparisons: the mountains beyond Borrowdale, 'bright and *washed*', as Coleridge said in a notebook, and Saddleback, quiet, 'no noise but that of the loose stones rolling away from the feet of the sheep that move slowly along the perilous ledges' under 'sun and clouds, with a thousand shadows on the hills'. More than once, I stopped over in Grasmere on the homeward journey, on the way to the boat-train to Liverpool, just to drive through a golden September dawn when the bracken was changing from green to gold, along that glorious road that Dorothy and William walked so often for the letters from Coleridge that did not come—the road from Grasmere to Ambleside.

Fairly early, luckily, in the summer of 1951, I reminded Routledge about the *Notebooks* clause in our *Inquiring Spirit* contract, and told them that I was now trying to clarify my plans for the editing. Their reply took the unexpected form of an invitation to lunch from Herbert Read, at that time a director of the firm. He took me to a good simple Italian restaurant not far from the British Museum (as always courteous in saving the other person's time) where the food was excellent and the air full of the thunder and lightning of Italian political talk, mostly, I gathered, anarchists arguing.

We plunged into Coleridge. I had screwed up my courage, determined to tackle Herbert Read on attributing existentialist views to Coleridge, a point he had made in *Coleridge as Critic*. His firm gentleness made courage unnecessary, but the argument did not end until our parting on the street corner. I see him there, hat gracefully lifted, the rain falling on his elegant grey head, still quietly arguing, but allowing me to have the last word; I was contending, I remember, that you might as well call Duns Scotus an existentialist as STC. I suppose I was against anachronistic definitions. And I had the temerity to object that Herbert was reading by existentialist hindsight into a passage in *The Friend* the existentialist horror of 'nothingness', whereas Coleridge was struck rather by awe than by horror, awe of the One, that *Vast* to which he became accustomed, the fullness, not the emptiness, of God. Years later I knew that we ought to have distinguished more clearly the conscious from the unconscious process. What counted for both of us, I think, was the way our minds worked with Coleridge, not our doctrines, and it was the first of many warm, illuminating, eye-catching encounters.

Intermittently we remembered the practical purpose for which we were met—to discuss the publishing of the Coleridge Note-books. He told me that they would be financially difficult if not impossible for a commercial publisher, and asked my permission to introduce the project to the Bollingen Foundation of New York. He would be seeing the Bollingen people in Eranos, Switzerland, the following week. As I had not heard of Bollingen before, he explained in the most general terms that it was a charitable founda-tion devoted to research enterprises of certain sorts, including the publication of commercially unviable books, such as the English translation of Jung's works, which Routledge had begun and which Bollingen was now sponsoring. In the detached spirit of Bollingen he did not enlarge on the personal details which I learned only much later, of how Bollingen, named after Jung's home in Switzer-land, was founded by Paul Mellon in memory of his first wife, Mary, the result of discussions with her and her friends, and reflecting her special concerns. Herbert told me that if the Bollin-gen people were interested, I should be asked to supply a descrip-tion of the material in the Notebooks and to suggest a budget for research needs; this would be followed, if this report met with a positive response, by talks in New York.

In October 1951 I sent in the requested statement proposing a complete edition of the Coleridge Notebooks, and describing the material:

'Nearly seventy notebooks were filled by S.T. Coleridge from 1794–1834, that is from a year before his marriage until his death. These have been inaccessible to scholars and are therefore largely unpublished. They are neither commonplace books nor diary, but something of both; they contain notes on literary, philosophical, scientific, social and psychological problems; anecdotes, plans for and fragments of works; comments on con-temporary persons and events; and many out-of-the-way items.

The widely accepted view of Coleridge as a fitful genius and frustrated poet, destroyed by metaphysics, procrastination and opium, would be revised by the publication of the notebooks.

His contemporaries, earlier editors, and the nineteenth century generally, failed to see his work whole. His awareness of psychological factors in every area of thought and experience, individual and social, was a hundred years ahead of his time. The notebooks reveal an arduous mental life, full of prophetic imagination and analytical acumen. They are not just another Coleridge work; they present not any one aspect, but an intimate and central approach to any understanding of Coleridge.'

Then I tried to describe the nature of the job, though it was impossible to convey the state of the notebooks; used from both ends and from the middle; gaps of as much as twenty-three years between entries on one page; passages quoted without identification, sometimes in the original language, sometimes translated or adapted; a private hodge-podge.

'The notebooks run to rather more than a million words and the entries are in chaos. They need to be put in chronological order. There was no sort of system, chronological or topical; and the first and most difficult and most time-consuming task, after the transcription, is the dating and ordering of the entries. Some of the writing is difficult—faded pencil, rain and sea water stains, careless writing, one entry superimposed on another, entries in cypher, these are some of the difficulties. Other problems require the help of persons with special knowledge of recondite Greek, German, and Italian, and the history of science and theology. The resources of the largest libraries will be required.'

I was able to say that from the photographs permitted by Geoffrey Coleridge and paid for by the Carnegie Foundation and the Leverhulme I had been able to go ahead with the transcription even through the war years, and that it was now in almost complete typescript. The cost of the typing, largely done before the war when prices—but also salaries—were much lower, I had borne myself. (It is shocking now to think of the miserable ten dollars a notebook that seemed to a friend an acceptable typing fee at a time of excruciatingly low wages.) Grants in aid of literary research were not common in those days, and I had been unable to find financial support in Canada. There was no alternative but to carry on the work as far as possible personally, in the confidence that its value would thus be easily demonstrable at a later stage. I hoped this would now be the case. In any event, the work itself had sustained me in this decision, even though I could not see the end of the road or even a turning.

As to the size of the work proposed, my guess was six to eight volumes, a brief preface, a literatim text and notes; entries and notes were to be numbered in chronological order, but with tables in the rear by which the curious reader could reconstruct a note-book if he so wished to by putting the entries back into their place on the pages. This idea arose from an argument with an English Coleridgean, Lawrence Hanson, who seriously wished to see the notebooks, spilled out one by one, just as they are—a view with which I sympathized in a way, but which to anyone who takes a good look at the manuscripts would obviously be thought a mad compounding of confusion. Some day perhaps someone will do it photographically, for scholars, but it will not be me.

What, they had asked, would I need? The largest item in my budget was for research assistance and a secretary-typist. (Corre-spondence about Coleridge had begun to overwhelm me, now that rumours about notebooks were in the wind.) And I should need travelling expenses to whatever libraries housed Coleridge collec-tions. There were more details about research methods, financial arrangements, applications for fellowships, and a wildly optimistic guess at how long the whole work would take.

Not long after my report and proposals went in, the invitation came to go to New York for talks. I am not sure, but I think it occasioned my first flight.

I shall not forget my first meeting with the chief officers of Bollingen Foundation, Jack Barrett and Vaun Gillmor at 140 East 62nd Street.

Jack Barrett was charming, a thinking, interested listener, with God knows what going on in his head, but as kind as he was enigmatic, a tactful, unhurried, wise person. Vaun Gillmor was a trifle alarming—tall, elegantly dressed, a woman socially experi-enced with an air of being securely *comme il faut*. I could not at first quite make out her function, but sensed that it was a signifi-cant one. These two people managed to dispel the formal aspects of the occasion and to carry on a delightful, seemingly irrelevant talk about both cabbages and kings. In fact there were times, not only at this first meeting but in later years during London visits, when they would crash into a busy British Museum day with an uproarious lunch—when I wondered whether we should ever get round to our Coleridge problems at all. Yet somehow, by the end of two or three hours' gaiety the problems were solved, understanding clarified and a great shot in the arm had been administered. Most publishers do a good deal of business while eating and drinking. Perhaps the making of books raises the subtler, more delicate personal, temperamental, issues that are best smoothed out by generosity and hospitality. At the good light-hearted talk that so stimulates that game, Vaun was an adept, and I came to realize that her rôle was also a solid practical down-to-earth one, and that she cared as deeply as Jack for the whole Bollingen enterprise and its standards. But on that first day I was not quite prepared for all those high spirits in such a context. Vaun's laughter and nonsense continued—to leaven any lumpish lapses into exaggerated anxiety or personal tension.

On that first occasion we went to some rather grand restaurant. I forget which one, but not any of the more intimate little favourites of later visits. I recall some conversation about my hotel, 'The Little Hotel' on 51st Street. It was falling down, and full of old residents who had been there for decades it seemed, and there was a good deal of nonsensical hilarity among us about such little hotels, and common agreement on their superiority to the big shiny new ones. In the shinier one in which we were lunching I had had one of those huge American fruit salads and noticed (just in time) a fat green caterpillar lurking under a lettuce leaf. It was not difficult to skirt him and he did not bother me, but as the waiter cleared my plate I could see that Jack spied it. We avoided each other's eyes but I felt we had both passed a couple of small tests. Back on 62nd Street, after another hour or more of discussion, his kindly amused smile as I took my leave remains vividly in my mind.

'There is just one more thing I should like to say, Miss Coburn. You have sent in a budget. Bollingen revises its budget every three years and I want you to know that if the Bollingen Board adopts a project, we see it through to the end. Do not worry about your first rough estimate. All very hypothetical, I know.'

What he really meant was that my budget was extremely naive.

But I was so sure that all would be well that I treated myself to a magnificent New York dinner that night.

Until Herbert Read introduced Coleridge and me to Bollingen, my picture of the publication of the Coleridge *Notebooks* was a hazy one, and lay so far in the future beyond mountain ranges of work, that the mere printing of pages was the least of my concerns. Bollingen put a Rolls-Royce under the whole thing. It was no longer just cart and carthorse. Having been rebuffed by the Oxford University Press and put off more gently by Cambridge, at some point I had discussed the possibility of publication with Jonathan Cape. He showed me the *Notebooks of Leonardo da Vinci*, produced by him in 1938 in two huge fat ugly volumes on paper nearly as thick as blotting paper, in a huge type I found very unsuitably blatant for notebook material. He was a wonderfully agile and alert man, but somehow, humourlessly perhaps, I did not find him congenial to Coleridge and me. He had a sense of fun and adventure though, as I was to see one night in Toronto a few years later when I watched him insist, after a concert, on consuming a revolting combination of waffles and Coca Cola because he had heard so often about both and had never tasted them. But as a businessman in his office he made me wary. I assumed, from then onwards, having no doubts whatever about the intrinsic value of the material itself and its eventual acceptance somewhere, that the thing for me to do was to prepare a volume before showing it to anyone else.

What Bollingen did was to confirm my confidence in the material and my approach to it, and to give a great fillip to the energy behind it by providing funds for secretarial and research assistance as well as publication. At every step since Bollingen entered the picture I have been aware that without its help any full-scale publication of the Coleridge *Notebooks* would have been impossible. Their faith in the project and their willingness to trust my judgement gave me the tools, and access to 'learneder clerks than I' provided the assurance that it could be completed. From the beginning, it was evident that the Coleridge expedition would not be a one-man affair or a one-woman one either. It was equally clear that Coleridge could not be edited by committee. The most sympathetic and variously learned experts would be needed to pursue his immense and often recondite reading in Greek, Latin, Hebrew, German and Italian. No school knowledge, or mere undergraduate training in any of these, would be enough; of Greek, Hebrew, and Italian I had none, and no belated hasty attempt to learn them would be adequate. Other pitfalls appeared as the work progressed. The topography of the English Lakes, for instance, was for a climber, and one with a special knowledge of the history of place-names; an historian of science would be needed for the later period, when Coleridge read avidly the new manuals of chemistry as they appeared and tried himself to invent a chemical vocabulary. A special kind of theologian would be needed also. As it proved, one of the most rewarding confessions in the world is the confession of ignorance. Help, asked for or proffered, has constituted some of the happiest parts of the enterprise. Few editors can have been luckier, and I wish it were possible adequately to convey in print the extent to which the editing has been teamwork.

In late August or September, 1951, on a brief holiday back on the island before term began, out of the Georgian Bay blue came a letter from A.P.Rossiter.

8.VIII.51	Jesus, Cambridge.

'Dear Miss Coburn,

I wonder whether you can help me over a question which has arisen in my mind from reading Item 186 in *Inquiring Spirit*. I know from experience that much, if not most, of the correspondence drawn by one's publications is from crazy persons; & in case you have found that too, I had better begin by showing that my form of derangement is a simple & predictable one. My queries will probably show that I am no S.T.C.-scholar; but I am a Cambridge don and a rock-climber, with a literary-critical interest in the development of aesthetic attitudes towards mountains between the late 17th century & the 19th, and for some years I have made a practice of going & seeing—or trying to see —the places which are described in Gray's Journal, Gilpin, West's Guide (1776) and so on.

Consequently I was extremely interested by Coleridge on Scafell...'

AP's later queries showed that he was indeed an 'STC scholar', and our correspondence was made voluminous by the painstaking care with which he not only answered my questions about place-names in the Lake District but proposed and answered a multitude of questions I was too ignorant to ask. He pored over maps, the photographs of the notebooks, the records and publications of the English Place Names Society, and made local inquiries when he could go to see the places themselves. All this, especially coming at the early stages when I was trying to produce a lucid typescript of text and notes, was invaluable; he capped it all finally by taking my printed galleys up Scafell on strenuous climbs with his wife, Barbara Bloch, in consequence of which he sent long corrections and detailed notes.

In addition, Rossiter had a degree in chemistry, and elucidated many of Coleridge's notes on Humphry Davy's first chemistry lectures at the Royal Institution in 1802. Most of the chemistry professors known to me would not touch it, the language being so outdated as to be quite foreign to them, but AP loved words, and the history of all words, from obscure antiquated chemical terms to obsolete Lake District names, and with typically energetic generosity he tackled my problems connected with them.

Coleridge's ascent of Scafell in 1802, and most particularly his descent, is famous among climbers for its vigour and its daring; he recorded it in Notebook 2 for Sara Hutchinson, but as he was new to much of the terrain his details left some unanswered questions. AP wrote (3 November 1952):

'We climbed Scafell twice in a week, and the little problem of the Way-down was most admirably illustrated by a trio of walkers; who were only too plainly making exactly the assumption that C. did, and arriving at the same predicament. I let them down like sacks on my rope, since they lacked C's nerve over "dropping from precipices". The rest of his way to "Taws" is amazingly unchanged. Not only is the "little village of sheep-folds" there, but even those stones or "hovels", he wasn't sure which, with grass, heather and mountain-ashes on top—we have a photograph of the one where "I am resting my book on one of its ledges . . . —tho it is NOT "a rival of Bowder" . . . You remember how he remarks on "the force of imitation in the Gardens . . . everywhere clipped yews, in obelisks and fine arches" between Torver and Coniston? [CN I 1228]. To my great surprise, there are at least half a dozen gardens in just this style, visible as you drive along the road . . . Another amusing little point concerns Devoke Water. I utterly disbelieved my reading of two words as "boat house" [CN I 1225]: thought it must be "peat-house"—for who on earth would build a boat-house in such a place?—None the less, there is a boathouse, and a photograph to prove it. The seabirds, however, are no longer in residence; though one of the 19th C. guidebooks mentions them —I forget which.'

His passion for accuracy at whatever cost to himself or anybody else, came out in his letters, sometimes with witty ferocity:

'Dear Kathleen,
   I wonder if you could possibly look up the files mentioned in your last letter and let me have the call-mark of the Ms. of *Confessions of an Inq. Spirit*? . . . I have for some time contemplated a systematic collection of errors of fact in writers on Coleridge, intended to demonstrate that there was a kind of contagious curse of factual inaccuracy which touched them all, sooner or later . . . It gets daily plainer to me that this unhappy man was not only—unlike Falstaff—witless in himself, but the cause that witlessness is in other men. Is it conceivable . . .'

And on he went about de Selincourt's mistakes, mine, and his own.

Until a few weeks before his death in a road accident in December 1956, despite physical miseries ('I seem almost Coleridgeanly unwell to-day, confound it,' he wrote in his last note), AP worked arduously to set me straight and to get Coleridge right. He did not see the finished result of his work in the first volume of the *Notebooks*, which came out in the next year, and consequently he must not be charged with any errors of mine: I was deprived of that letter of jubilation and fault-finding to which I had eagerly looked forward.

AP had been a Cambridge pupil of I.A.Richards. I did not meet Richards until the Christmas vacation of 1951 in the other Cambridge, in Massachusetts, but I had heard him lecture in Oxford in 1931, and had written a cheeky review of his *Coleridge on Imagina-*

tion in 1934. That had been for me exactly the right book at the right time, gritty, ardent, direction-pointing without fetishes. In the Christmas vacation of 1951 there he was, just across the corridor in the same apartment block in Arlington Street, Cambridge, Mass., taking me seriously. Having read *Inquiring Spirit* and *The Philosophical Lectures*, he was full of questions about them, and about Coleridge. As I remember our first meetings they were all questions and few answers—not a bad beginning for what has been for me, in the true sense, a wonderfully enriching relationship. Help comes in various forms.

VII

1952

This was the warmest London summer I had ever experienced, but then each London summer seemed better than the previous one. There was my usual visit to Ottery, which Geoffrey Coleridge called 'a shattering prospect',

> '... If you come to see us you will find a pair of tottering & ageing relicts & must treat us gently. This summer I retire from Bench & shall no longer deal with law breakers as under a new regulation all magistrates are put on a "supplemental" list at the age of 75. So you see how decrepit I am considered to be! Gilbert C has just become 93 which is a bit cheering however. May 1952 be a happy one for you is the wish of
>
> Yrs affec: C'

Geoffrey's uncle, Gilbert Coleridge, was always indeed more than a bit cheering. Aged ninety-three, he had been, I believe, an active magistrate until a year or two before. Though not in the main march of my story, he is worth recording in himself, and certainly he was one of the extra dividends from work on STC. I have forgotten which member of the family introduced me to Gilbert and Winifred Coleridge, but somehow I had been invited to tea in Haverfield House on Kew Green in 1948–9.

Gilbert Coleridge was the oldest surviving member of his generation, the youngest son of John Duke Coleridge, the Lord Chief Justice of England and first baron. He was the only person I was likely to meet who knew someone (his father) who had seen Coleridge. There were no useful research consequences from this, just the pleasure of the human fact itself. He was a character, a man of the world who had travelled the law circuits with his father, went to the United States with him, and boasted of having danced down Broadway with Ellen Terry. He was a water-diviner and had

located several wells. He was also a founder of the Richmond Ice
Rink and the last time I saw him he was cursing vehemently two
acquaintances who a few months before had insisted on seeing him
home after a fall on the ice. 'Of course the damn fools gave the
whole thing away and I had to promise Winifred not to skate any
more. You can't blame her. She has her ninety-five year-old
mother upstairs with a broken hip—she doesn't want another
invalid.'

I think it may have been on the same visit that, tidying up his
papers and trying to dispose of certain things, he tossed a batch of
clippings out of a drawer—book reviews he had written in court.
He explained that on circuit with his father he often had little to do
during large parts of the proceedings and could read books and
even write reviews of them. One he pulled out, of *Tess of the
D'Urbervilles*, he was proud of, as well he might be. He had written
appreciatively of it on its first appearance in 1891, when the general
chorus of the critics attacked it on moral grounds.

He loved hearing of anything that seemed to him physically
adventurous, and I remember one tea-time in the garden of Haverfield House when he bored everyone around us with interminable
questions about my Georgian Bay island, everything from bears,
visible or not, to 'those dear little old oil lamps'. To paddle a canoe
through hundreds of miles of northern lakes and forests seemed to
be his life's unfulfilled ambition.

At the age of seventy, hand untrained and eyesight failing, he had
taken up sculpture, partly because he was incensed that there was
no effigy of S.T.Coleridge in Ottery St Mary. He did a head, in
low relief, over it an albatross, and below it the verse:

> 'He prayeth best, who loveth best
> All things both great and small;
> For the dear God who loveth us,
> He made and loveth all.'

I could not tell him that STC himself had expressed doubts about
the appropriateness of these lines.

The bronze portrait is not very good, but the generosity of spirit
behind it, and the genuine love of creative activity—for it was this
and not mere vanity about the family name that dictated the

gesture—endears it on other than artistic grounds. His autobiography, *Some and Sundry*, does not seem to me to come up to
his letters to me, which were voluminous, sometimes witty, and
always lively.

In the summer of 1952 I apparently kept no record of events;
nor have letters survived. It was in fact so hectic a summer, the
first with a paid research assistant who had to be broken in, and so
much scribbling was going on day after day in the British Museum,
that probably little went in other directions. Unresolved problems
in annotating the material to go into the first volume (the hardest
nuts left uncracked from earlier failures in the search) were my
main preoccupation; they had nearly all been tried also by various
experts. As the deadline of the end of the summer vacation approached, the atmosphere became quite frantic—sources un-
located, datings uncertain, readings still mysterious after many
trips to the Manuscript Room of the British Museum, haunting
suspicions of concealed allusions. But then occasionally the horrific
pits of potential error that opened at one's feet would give way to
delight as answers popped up here and there. The putting of wits
together over our sandwich and half a bitter in the Plough, or the
Bull & Mouth, or The Crown, the endless questions, the frank
brain-picking of relative strangers, was and is part of the cheerfulness of research that swirls in and out of the Museum generally,
but Coleridge seems to induce a particular brand of this gaiety, and
open, generous talk.

One person who shared with me the agonies and the little daily
triumphs of this hectic time was Elizabeth Mary Wilkinson, who
had undertaken to pursue the numerous and difficult German
entries. When I was leaving Canada in 1948 for a year in England,
I asked my dear friend (and sometimes dear combatant) Barker
Fairley, a transplanted Yorkshireman turned ardent Canadian,
where to look for a Germanist. 'Ask Leonard Willoughby,' he
said. 'He knows everyone in German worth knowing, and besides,
he is the sort of person who will take thought to find the *right* one.'
And so it proved, exactly as he said. Leonard Willoughby introduced me to another bit of Yorkshire, Mary Wilkinson.

Mary shared my enjoyment of these crazy pursuits and participated in the mounting pressures of that summer of 1952 and
others that followed. The great blessed moments were those when

once in a while we each climbed down whatever particular tree we were up at the time and, with a mixture of ecstasy and desperation, groaned and purred over what we saw of the whole wood. In harmony, in argument, cheerfully, furiously, we knocked our heads together; for there was in it all that combination of zest for solutions, daemonic concentration, and personal affection that makes such working together one of the most honest privileges and some of the best fun in the human world.

I remember particularly one day—it may have been in the next summer—seeing Mary as white as a sheet, shaking from head to foot, breathless beside my seat in the North Library. 'Look!' she said. '*Is* this his hand?' She had brought in from the main reading room—how she got past the doorman we never knew, for it is strictly against the rules to carry volumes from one room to another —a copy of Kant's *Grundlegung zur Metaphysik der Sitten*. By good luck, or perhaps intuition, she had ordered out the fourth edition, published in Riga in 1797. It was then catalogued like any ordinary book, with no reference in the catalogue to the pencilled markings she found in the margins. There on p. 54 were the initials, 'S.T.C. Decemb. 6. 1803, Keswick'. And the neighbouring pages of Kant provided such pointed and rich solutions to some difficult entries in Notebook 16 that she was reeling with excitement. But did I feel 'certain it *was* his hand?' (There was no doubt in my mind.) And 'how sharp he was in his criticism here of Kant, attacking Kant's limited metaphors, bringing in Schiller by contrast,' and so on and on. Many interesting links began to click into place; the results are to be seen in Notebooks Volume I, entries 1705, 1717 and 1723.

The intensity of the work and the pleasure from it would have been immeasurably less without Mary's knowledge and curiosity, her tenacity when the landfalls were hard to come by, her awareness of psychological and aesthetic subleties, her love of style, and her generous outspokenness. Like a good Yorkshire terrier, she took between her teeth the German entries in the Coleridge notebooks and shook them until they yielded their meaning. Sometimes with, sometimes without, envy, I thought often times that no scholar had any right to be so brainy and so beautiful.

As if the work itself was not enough for that summer, towards the end of it an unexpected little drama took place of quite another sort. It had to do with the purchase from A.H.B.Coleridge

of his S. T. Coleridge collection for Victoria College, part of the
collection I had first seen in the library of his father, the Reverend
Gerard Coleridge in Leatherhead in 1931. He had died in 1945, and
Alwyne, the eldest son, a solicitor, had most of his father's collection in his possession.

When after the war Alwyne was settled in a small house in
Epsom, the S.T.Coleridge material he inherited was, when I saw it,
on shelves and in a great chest under the dining table. He complained of the sheer bulk of STC and also of the quantity of expensive and time-consuming correspondence to which it gave rise.
AHB could be a very gracious man, but he was, I thought, much
burdened by his awareness of the greatness of the family in the past,
and by responsibilities which therefore sat heavily on him. He was
shrewd, and always had more interest in S.T.Coleridge and more
knowledge of his work than he cared to display. He was a bit like
Geoffrey Coleridge in chaffing one constantly, sometimes rudely,
sometimes cleverly, so that it was an event to go to see him. There
were many visits to him over several years, and a considerable
correspondence with me exists which shows his knowledge of the
STC circle and his willingness to put it, and his legal training, at
the service of Coleridge scholars. It was he, for instance, who first
grasped the importance of a transcript of notes of Coleridge's
early lectures on Natural and Revealed Religion, and early in the
summer of 1952 he lent me the manuscript in his grandfather's
hand, and gave permission to have it copied. As the original had
disappeared, this was the only text of Coleridge's first series of
public lectures, lectures given in 1795.

Coleridge's books and manuscripts on his death were divided
for editorial purposes among three persons, his friend Joseph
Henry Green, who was to deal with the philosophical manuscripts—such as the *Philosophical Lectures*, the *Logic*, the *Opus
Maximum*—his nephew and son-in-law, Henry Nelson Coleridge,
who had the poems and the literary lectures and fragments—and
the second son, Derwent, who had responsibility for theological
works and related marginalia and fragments. On Green's death in
1845, and on Sara's in 1851, their collections went to Derwent, and
in succession to his son, Ernest Hartley, then to his son the Rev.
Gerard of Leatherhead and then, what was left after various
depletions, to his son A.H.B.Coleridge, the solicitor. Sections of

material had been lopped off occasionally from early times. E.H. Coleridge in the eighteen nineties sold much of the manuscript material to the British Museum. At some point, in need of finding money to send his eldest son to Cambridge, he formed the plan of selling to his cousin, the Lord Chief Justice of England, John Duke Coleridge, some fifty-five notebooks and nearly two hundred of STC's books, with letters and some other papers. EHC spent days and nights for years transcribing from the notebooks, doubtless preparatory to the life of S.T.Coleridge which he intended to write. Volumes of his transcripts, and transcripts by other hands (mostly ladies he referred to as his 'literary concubines'), became part of G.H.B. Coleridge's inheritance. In fact G.H.B.Coleridge's collection contained a dozen notebooks, and more than a hundred books owned (some annotated) by Coleridge, letters, the *Philosophical Lectures* and other manuscripts, the so-called *Opus Maximum*, a manuscript of *Christabel* made for Sara Hutchinson, but in addition a considerable conglomeration of materials sent to the family editors or collected by them—manuscripts of Southey, Charles Lamb, Wordsworth, clippings, reviews, and many a curious oddment saved by the family. They either recognized very early the importance of their greatest ancestor, or they had a magpie in the genes. I suppose G.H.B.Coleridge's collection was never so valuable as it was before the lot was sold by his father to the first Lord Coleridge, but when I first saw what there was of it in the 1930s it was still a very considerable one.

In 1943, when Gerard Coleridge, ill with tuberculosis, was about to move to Cornwood in Devon, his books were divided into three categories, A, B and C. A was to be retained in the family; C was to be offered to Blackwell; B, a borderline group, was to be open for discussion. Two men went down from Blackwell to select them. Actually when the books were removed, so the late Rev. Anthony Coleridge told me, not only did group C go, but too many of B, and even some A books. His father was too ill to cope. There were two sales in which scores of items disappeared.

Some years later, in this summer of 1952, A.H.B.Coleridge was ill, living in Epsom, forced to give up his legal work, and anxious to go to Devon, the Coleridge county, to begin raising poultry. He had written to an American Coleridgian, he told me, asking what his STC collection would fetch in the United States, but he had had no response. He had been to Sotheby's, made some inquiries of a clerk, but felt brushed off. I suggested the British Museum, and perhaps the Pilgrim Trust again, and had his permission to inquire. The answer from the Museum was negative. They had no funds for Coleridge, nor would the officials of the day sanction another appeal to the Pilgrim Trust. The Keeper of Manuscripts, no longer Mr Skeat, was not greatly interested in Coleridge and implied he could think of better uses for Pilgrim Trust money. In the ups and downs of that summer of ill-health, AHBC finally muttered, walking down an Epsom road and kicking a stone a great way ahead of him as he did so, 'Oh, if somebody would give me x—thousand pounds I'd sell the *lot*." And he hoisted me into a bus.

Once again, as at Ottery six years before, my excitement was mounting during the last few days before sailing for home. No time to lose. On the train I wrote a letter to an old friend, Arthur Meighen, twice our Canadian Prime Minister, but now retired from politics. He loved English literature, and always plied me with questions whenever we met, not only about Coleridge's views on Shakespeare, with which he often disagreed, but about my work on the notebooks. We read and discussed many a passage together. He was pleased about the sale of Lord Coleridge's collection to the British Museum, of which he had had a blow-by-blow account, and he would, I knew, trust my experience with that sale as enabling me to form some judgement of the value of this smaller collection. He was the one person I knew well enough to approach, who (as I told him) had enough money and sufficient power of quick decision to lend me the sum at once, on my total non-security. It was a Saturday, and the letter was posted between train and theatre. Wednesday morning I was wakened by a cablegram being pushed under my door in the hotel: 'Sterling funds sent. Good luck. AM.' After the British Museum's refusal, my plan was to buy the collection and then find a donor to give it to the Victoria College Library in the University of Toronto. The reason for urgency was A.H.B. Coleridge's unstable state of health, and the fear as before that if an institution was not its destination, an auction sale might scatter to the four winds a collection much of the value of which lay in its being held together.

But before I could ring up Alwyne and tell him I had his required number of pounds, tact and delicacy required holding off until I had written, as I had promised Bollingen to do but had procrastinated in doing, to ask him to renew formally his father's permission to me to edit the notebooks. I was afraid the purchase price of the collection might appear to be a bribe, and it seemed essential to keep these separate things distinct. I wrote and received the reply that 'my father's unqualified permission still holds good'.

The next day I rang him up to tell him I had the amount he had specified, and that if he agreed to the Victoria College library having the collection, I would give him the bank draft. His excitement was vibrant through the telephone. Could I get to Epsom that afternoon —for lunch?

In view of the British Museum's rejection of the collection, I was able to put up a strong case for acquisition by a university library in Canada. The war was not long behind us, and Canadian troops had swarmed about Leatherhead. Alwyne knew some of them, his father married many of them to English girls, and there was still alive in England generally some sense of obligation to Canada for standing by Britain from the moment war was declared, two years before the United States got into the war. If the British Museum was so stuffy, Alwyne said, then why not Canada? If England could have Canadian troops, why should Canada not have a few English literary manuscripts?

The price he set, when the pound was still at par, was considered a reasonable one at that time, in the light of the carefully estimated price of the Chanter's House collection. Because of a condition of secrecy imposed by Alwyne, and also because the full extent of the collection was not precisely known, even by me, it was impossible to discuss it with anyone. The sale was conducted in a most gentlemanly and unbusiness-like manner. I simply accepted his view of what should be considered the S.T.Coleridge material. Other things which he categorized as belonging to Sara or Hartley or Derwent I did not argue about. For instance, a copy of Hartley Coleridge's *Northern Worthies* with STC's holograph notes in it, three volumes, was in my view more relevant nowadays to STC than to his son, but Alwyne naturally attached it to Hartley; it would have created tension, perhaps held up the whole transaction, to have insisted on having it. I trusted him implicitly when he said that, 'if any more STC stuff turned up', he would send it to us.

So on September 3, Alwyne agreed to the sale and we had a happy afternoon talking over the collection, the public service he was doing by not dispersing the lot at auction, the value to Canadian students of having original manuscripts to study, and the relief to him of loosing this albatross from his neck. He was interested to hear about Arthur Meighen, likewise a man of law, and that a person of such eminence was interested enough in STC to finance the purchasing of his collection for a college library was, in a way, a further consolation and justification. It was clear that the sale was not easy for him, when it came down to the fine thing. 'What will old —— say!' he kept chortling. This was an embarrassment to me, as 'old ——' was working in the British Museum at the time and I was constantly showing him notebook material—in fact we lived in hotels opposite each other on Montague St and the porters in each got used to the repeated exchanges of bundles of typescript across the street. It would have been natural to discuss the collection with him, and the price, but I was sworn particularly not to disclose Alwyne's plans. After all, he said, he had invited 'old ——' to help him sell it through some American bookseller and 'old ——' had done nothing. There was a slight huff in the air.

We agreed that a licence to export was essential.

'Ask old —— how you do it! He has done it before, but don't let him know what's up!' Alwyne loved being obstreperous.

I went back up to London, called the Board of Trade to find out the procedures, postponed by a week my sailing fixed for the following Saturday and cabled the college that I should be late for term, asking them to send the necessary customs forms for valuables destined for a public institution. My research assistant at that time, Oliver Stonor, went off with me to railway left-luggage shops to buy the five tough old suitcases we thought would be suitable. He kindly jumped on each one that was offered, to make sure that it would be strong enough to hold very precious books. We walked along Oxford St rather like circus clowns, carrying the enormous unsightly cases which were to become objects of further mirth with various taxi drivers and railway porters before I was finally poured out of a taxi with all of them at Alwyne's door in Epsom on Friday, September 5.

I was armed also with Mr Meighen's banker's order, and export forms supplied by the Board of Trade which we both had to sign.

Alwyne went off to his bank and deposited the money, returning in a fine state of cheerfulness. I had thought perhaps his wife and I could be doing some of the packing in the meantime, but no, it was clear that he wished to hand me the books, a few at a time, looking carefully at each one. We put the notebooks, the manuscript of *Christabel*, and other Grade A matter into two of the best of the cases, stateroom luggage which I could keep with me during the whole voyage (much as Joanna had slept over her most precious manuscripts in the blitzes). The rest were quickly stowed in the other cases and I was back in London that evening, but alas not in time to take the export forms to the Board of Trade. I recall 'old ——' coming over to dine with me in my hotel that Sunday, a painful dinner for me because of having to keep Alwyne's secret; my notes made a few days later on shipboard tell me that we discussed the hypothetical financial value of the collection and that his views were reassuring on the fairness of the price looked at from both sides.

The next week another hair-raising little flurry ensued. Saturday, 13, I was to sail. On Monday, September 8, I took the completed forms to the Board of Trade. On Wednesday a necessary 'CD3' form from Alwyne's bank arrived and everything seemed in order. On Thursday, by very exceptional chance leaving the British Museum and going back to the hotel for something in mid-afternoon, I found an urgent message from the secretary to the signing officer in the Board of Trade. The forms must be typed in triplicate, each case of manuscripts to be listed separately, and she hinted that I might still have to do some talking to get permission to export. Loyally, in the firm way of friendship, Anne Renier typed half the night so that I could get the forms to the Board of Trade first thing Friday morning. The Board of Trade official was very shy about signing anything to do with manuscripts. Farm implements, now, they were his cup of tea. He was not in his secretary told me, but could I hold myself available in an hour's time to see him if there were doubts? The Board of Trade closed at four on Friday. My ship sailed at midnight Saturday from Southampton. What I did not dare utter to anyone was that the three or four luggage-in-advance cases were possibly already in Southampton, perhaps in the hold of the ship.

My desk in the British Museum was still littered with unsolved problems and part-solutions, but instinct told me that if I had a difficult diplomatic mission ahead of me with the Board of Trade, I should take the time to buy a new hat. Early on Friday morning I rushed off to Heath's, then in Oxford St, and found a quite pretty one, still affectionately remembered. It should have been preserved for the Victoria College archives; perhaps it did the trick.

My official was very worried. So was I. The morning was slipping by in talk. I suggested that as the Department of Manuscripts in the British Museum was the signing authority for the National Trust, perhaps he would like me to take the forms round and ask them to sign them—there would just be time to go in a cab and get back before lunch. (He would not be available after that.) 'That is more than kind of you, I'm sure,' his secretary heard him say, to her great amusement as she returned to the room. There was barely time, but fortunately the right person was there in the Department of Manuscripts, who knew that I had done my best to persuade the Museum to buy the collection; permission, as I believe he pointed out to superior powers, could hardly be refused me. The signed papers in my hand, hat at a more rakish angle no doubt, I raced back to the Board of Trade. That was 12.30. At 2.00 his secretary, whose name I much regret having forgotten but not my gratitude to her, rang to say the licence to export was ready. I picked it up on the way to Epsom for a farewell tea hour. I found that Alwyne had roped all the cases as he promised, had indeed sent off the Grade B and C bags to the ship, paid the insurance, hounded the transport company, all most helpfully and efficiently.

A mild aftermath to all this was to take place in *The Times*, but just now there was no time to think of anything but those unanswered questions on my desk. I had but Saturday morning.

In the midst of those all but insupportably hectic little *rencontres*, almost in the last hour in the Museum before catching the boat train, there was another incredibly lucky dip. Humphry House has told the story in part in an Appendix to his Clark Lectures on Coleridge, but he could hardly convey the increase in my pulse rate. rate.

He had once asked me if I knew the source of an entry in Notebook 21 which Coleridge had used in the fifteenth chapter of *Biographia Literaria*, where he coined his famous adjective for Shakespeare, 'myriad-minded'. Coleridge's footnote there reads:

'*Ἀνὴρ μυριόνους*, a phrase which I have borrowed from a Greek monk, who applies it to a Patriarch of Constantinople . . .'

In *Anima Poetae* (a small selection from the notebook entries edited by Coleridge's grandson, E.H.Coleridge) the entry as printed beclouds rather than clarifies the mysterious reference. *Anima Poetae* has to quote but a part:

'*Ο ΜΥΡΙΌΝΟΥΣ*—hyperbole from Naucratius panegyric of Theodorus Chersites. Shakespeare, *item*, . . .'

At the beginning of the summer, Humphry and I discussed the several puzzling aspects of all this, and found we had pursued exactly the same routes in our searches to exactly the same dead end. He was preparing his Clark Lectures of 1952 for the printer, and he wanted Coleridge's source for the phrase. It was some weeks later that, having noticed Coleridge referring to William Cave as a literary historian, and elsewhere to Cave on Duns Scotus, it struck me that if Cave was a useful historian for one mediaeval monk he might be for another and should be searched for Theodore. Being pressed with other problems, I asked my research assistant to go out to the open shelves (it was there then) to look at Cave's *Scriptorum Ecclesiasticorum Historia Literaria*. He, also pressing on with his own searches, said, 'Oh, I've had a look at old Cave a while ago. I don't think it's there.' Full of tense rage at his time-wasting resistance in this critical last-gasp moment, I raced out myself to the open shelves, and in a very few minutes Theodorus leapt out from the pages of Cave, as 'Theodorus, Studites à monasterio'. '*Studites*', not *Chersites*; it made sense. One good look at the notebook again established beyond doubt that Coleridge in fact wrote 'Studites'; EHC had mis-read the manuscript. Cave's article on St Theodore, Greek and Latin in parallel columns, explained the anomalies in *Biographia*, and also helped to correct the errors in the Greek, and in the interpretation in *Anima Poetae*. Correctly the entry reads, as it is now printed in the *Notebooks* I 1070. To use Humphry House's translation of the Greek phrases:

'The myriad-minded—hyperbole from Naucratius's panegyric of Theodorus Studites—Shakespeare?'

Thus in a flash total defeat in research turns into triumph. A nonsensical mystery is clarified by a lucky conjunction of doors opening. The key had to be found, in this case the book Coleridge had on his desk or in his mind; nothing short of this, no simple search among appropriate Greek monks, would do. I suppose a large part of the excitement in this sort of sleuthing—as perhaps in any sort—is the sense of the hairsbreadth by which one might have missed it, the single little stone not overturned, the page missed. Oliver had 'looked' at Cave, but not with this problem in mind. Anyhow, I recall that at the moment of discovery I had about half an hour to get to the bank for cash for my homeward journey, before the Saturday-morning closing time. In any case—and it was before the days of rapid-copying—I was too paralysed with ecstasy to transcribe accurately and had to ask Oliver to do it while I walked on air to the bank. He had the grace to do it with as much good will and pleasure as if he had found it himself.

Unfortunately there is an unhappy postscript to these exciting pleasures of the summer of 1952. Secrecy lifted, I wrote to Humphry House from aboard ship to tell him that the manuscript of the Theological Lectures, which I had made available to a post-graduate student of his for editing, was no longer in Epsom but could be available in Canada. (I had already had it transcribed, and the student, Peter Mann, had checked the transcript against the original.) I added in a P.S. that I had the solution of the 'Theodorus Chersites' problem, in my trunks in the baggage room, and would be glad to send it to him when I got home if there was still time for him to use it. Humphry was furious at not having been informed about the sale of the A.H.B. Coleridge Collection earlier. He wrote me a very angry letter, angry at not having been informed (as he considered his due after his co-operation in preparing the report for the Pilgrim Trust about the Ottery collection), suggesting that there would be some awkwardness now for his student Peter Mann with the Oxford Board, and saying with what I felt was childish petulance that he had met Lord Coleridge and had seen the note-books before I did, and that he had helped with the procuring of the Ottery collection because he believed in my policy of consolidat-ting Coleridge materials. He implied some diminution in my can-dour and goodwill, accusing me of mystery-making and undue secrecy. His P.S. said, 'No, thank you'. He did not now wish to have my solution to the Theodorus problem, he had 'not claimed to annotate in that way'. However, he reminded me that I had promised to check in galley-proof the text of his quotations from the notebooks, and as he would like 'to keep separate things distinct' he would still send them.

I am afraid I wrote an equally fierce reply, explaining the facts of the situation, that there was no deliberate mystery, that the British Museum had turned down my offer, that there was no alteration in regard to Mann's use of the manuscript, except that it would now be in a college library and more easily available. I also, rivalling his childishness, put the record straight as to priority in use of the notebooks which he had first seen in 1934, though I refrained from telling him that Lord Coleridge had asked me if House was a 'suitable fellow to allow in the house'. I expressed my gratitude for his help in the past, and ended the letter with a not altogether pacific paragraph:

'In due course the A.H.B. Coleridge Collection will be catalogued and available to scholars. We hope that some of you will come and work here at least on your way to the collections already in New York and California; if you do, the effective force of the manuscripts may be greater than if they had remained in Epsom. The world of scholarship is one, you know, and I am not going to allow it to be split by your wrath or mine at yours!'

When the snippets from Humphry's galley-proofs arrived—he did not send the complete set but had taken the trouble to excise the notebook quotations—the Theodorus passage was still full of the old mistakes. It was impossible, I felt, to go on propagating these silly errors when we now knew the right readings. I sent him a copy of my note, making the necessary corrections to his old version from *Anima Poetae*. Humphry was a scholar; at his best he could not let personal feelings stand in the way of truth. He wrote gratefully about this and the numerous other corrections, and in the end (as he was in page-proof by now) at Rupert Hart-Davis's suggestion, he wrote an Appendix to his book, telling in outline the story of my discovery in Cave.*

* See Humphry House, *Coleridge*: The Clark Lectures 1951–52 (Rupert Hart-Davis, London, 1953).

In October 1954 the J.S. MacLean Foundation of Toronto paid for the AHBC collection and presented it to the Victoria College Library in the University of Toronto, now known as the Victoria University Library. The collection has been constantly used by graduate students and visiting scholars from all over the world.

One small corollary, because it tells something characteristic about my old friend. Arthur Meighen did not treat casually, nor as a mere formality, my debt to him. Though I saw that it hurt him to accept those monthly instalments from me, he did nothing to stop them. After two years, when the MacLean Foundation paid the whole back to him, I was able to buy my first car with what he returned to me, savings in fact he had thus forcibly imposed on me. He admitted he had feared I was a trifle extravagant and thought he could help me to learn to save. A strong and staunch friend.

VIII

1953–1954

So now, after April 1952, the Coleridge Notebooks and I had the great boon of funds for assistance, a typist, an indexer, and an assistant in the research in the British Museum for a few weeks in my summers there. But it soon became evident that it would be necessary to see every Coleridge manuscript wherever it was. The use or meaning of cryptic entries could be made plain by a scrap of his lecture note in the Cornell library, or his annotation on some book in California. Harvard and Yale had some Coleridge manuscripts; and what was there in New York, or Cornell or Chicago? Or possibly in Vermont, where Dr Marsh had launched Coleridge in America? What might be scattered about in other libraries in England? Collections known and unknown had to be seen, and some long stretches of free time must be found. The notebooks being central to Coleridge's works, often the very adytum, it was necessary to search out all possible clues everywhere. I did not ask for, nor later when it was suggested accept, a Bollingen Fellowship, which would have meant giving up teaching. I was unwilling to forgo the life of the college and university community, and especially the at once sobering and heartening influence of the young. So for the next fifteen years I carried on with full-time teaching, applying for occasional fellowships, and after that, teaching half-time.

In the fall of 1952 my old skating companion of Oxford years, William Wallace, now an enthusiastic teacher of Classics in University College, Toronto, and himself a Guggenheim Fellow, proposed me for a Guggenheim Fellowship. It released me in 1953–4 for full-time research work. He was a friend who would take trouble for one (he taught me, *inter alia*, to drive a car), and many of my notes indirectly owe something to his fine gift for conversation. His death some years later, far too young, meant to me personally the loss of affection, frank criticism, and an invigorating companionship.

The spring and early summer of 1953 were a period of intense concentration, days usually sixteen hours long, in final preparation of the text and notes of the first volume of the Notebooks. Yet one discovers there is no such thing as 'final' where Coleridge is concerned. I remember a frantic communication from Mary Wilkinson. 'STOP. All those notes on the German word-lists in Notebook $3\frac{1}{2}$ are now useless.' These referred to entries made by Coleridge in Germany when he was beginning to learn German methodically. He had tried to make his notebook into a vocabulary book, not alphabetically but according to weird subject categories, with lists of words very strange indeed for a beginner's German. 'What I've told you about the words themselves is true enough,' she went on, 'but, Glory Hallelujah! I've found out where he got them! You'll *never* guess. They're all out of Bürger's translation of *Macbeth*!! What a *one* he was! What a way to learn his German!' In due course Mary's re-written notes came along.

I was now on to the real preparation of the manuscript of *Notebooks 1*, as I thought for approaching publication. The approach, however, was a very gradual uphill slope.

For those who are interested in processes, I record the trial-and-error method that was used. This was the first volume, and everything was an experiment. That 'the chronological order is the best', as Coleridge had said, I was sure, but it was less than certain that with the notebooks in chaos it could be satisfactorily presented. So in July what was sent off to New York was the text and notes for all material relevant to Volume One, plus uncertainties, from Notebooks Gutch, 1, 2, 3, 4, 5, $5\frac{1}{2}$, 6, 7, 8, 10, 16, 21—nearly three thousand entries, but still as they stood in each notebook, and not in their time order. I seem to remember that New York asked for them that way and borrowed the photographs to get on with checking my script. The re-ordering into a chronological sequence was left for September; by mid-July exhausted flesh would take no more.

Six weeks of sun and swimming and Georgian Bay peace—1953 was an unusually hot summer—worked the usual restoration. True, the proofs of *The Letters of Sara Hutchinson* had to be read; George and Elizabeth Whalley had generously taken on the indexing of them. The mornings were still sacred to work until noon, and the afternoons were full of the enterprises of the island—canoeing,

sometimes fishing of an afternoon, a bit of clearing away of under-
brush, blueberrying, the odd visit from Johnson Tabobandung
or his boys, and always the heavenly swimming. One hot day at
noon Wallace Brockway—'the man from Bollingen', we had been
calling him—suddenly appeared. A very pale and wan New
Yorker, very nervous of every single aspect of our northern
wilderness, he bravely came for three days to discuss technicalities
connected with the difficult eccentricities and inconsistencies confronting us in the notebooks. Wallace did nothing to reduce my
anxieties and labours over the Coleridge text, nor did I allay his
fears about snakes, porcupines, or raccoons he might meet on a
path. I remember on his arrival taking him down to the shore
thinking we might as well have a preliminary talk out in the sun and
air of which he seemed to be obviously in need, and that as I sat
down on a great slab of granite, Wallace pulled the finest lawn
handkerchief I had ever seen from his breast pocket and spread it
out under him. I protested that he had never in his life sat on anything so clean as that rock.

'Oh, it's not that, Kathleen. It's just that my pants are so thin!'
They were indeed, almost as fine as the handkerchief. After about
three minutes of sitting on that hard though hygienic granite,
hospitality dictated that we carry on our conversation indoors.

He had his innings when we began checking my typescript
against the photographs of the notebooks. After one long session, I
recall crossly throwing down my pencil over an interminable
argument about Coleridge's apostrophe S and S aspostrophe,
especially *its'* and *it's*, saying I refused to have a nervous break-
down making a million decisions as to whether his apostrophes
were east or west of his 's'. Wallace was fidgetting over each one,
usually in opposition to my decision in the typescript. By using a
fine ruler, he could sometimes demonstrate his case. But I remember equally with what charm he became placatory when I
finally said we should standardize them, and say so in the Introduction. 'Whatever you like, my dear, so long as we say so in the
Introduction.' Wallace could irritate one beyond speech, but at the
same time be a strength to another that he was not to himself. It
must be said that although he created problems, he was also invaluable as a critical consultant; his contribution to the Coleridge
work was as penetrating as it was infuriating. It was also witty,

learned, and sophisticated. I would not be without memories of Wallace, whose intellect entitled him to more distinction than his life allowed him.

By the autumn of 1953 the index was already begun, based on notebook and entry numbers, not as yet serialized. It was being prepared by a remarkable character, Gertrude Boyle. Indexing by notebook and entry numbers instead of waiting for page-proofs in the usual way proved invaluable in the ordering of the materials and in cross-referencing; in fact I do not see how the notebooks could have been produced without this advance form of indexing. Gertrude came up to the island for a week or two of work and consultation. She had retired as chief cataloguer of the Toronto Public Reference Library, where for thirty years or more she had trained most of the cataloguers in Canada. A fierce little lady with minute hands and feet that somehow raced over files or floor with startling rapidity, she had a splendid sense of humour and an equally splendid intolerance of inaccuracy—Coleridge's, mine, and everyone else's. We had great fun, some hot and bothered times, exasperated, weary times, but her goodwill and determination never flagged. At first her stern Puritan upbringing, or perhaps just a personal reserve, made her critical of one she regularly referred to as 'Mr Coleridge'. Why did 'Mr Coleridge' want to write down on paper, even for himself, all the things he did write? However, after a few months I heard that she was offering to others my arguments for the defence, and that her friends were setting conversational traps simply to provoke her into doing so. One day when I was driving her home in a thick blizzard through slow traffic that gave opportunity for ample talk, she made a characteristically honest confession of the softening influence of STC on her. In reporting someone's misfortunes or mistakes or unhappiness of some kind, she said, 'Well, it's really all her own fault . . .' and then stopped herself short. 'Oh, no,' she said, 'that's not true'. With a sheepish smile she turned to look me in the eye. 'Thanks to Mr Coleridge I don't think in that way any more.'

Perhaps a professional indexer (not the same breed as a cataloguer), given a free hand, would have prepared a better index. Some decisions taken then I should not take now. But the process Gertrude Boyle put me through in coming to the principles and practices we arrived at was more than worth the agony. She saved me, as good indexers do, from many slips, oversights, and down-right errors. Illness overtook her towards the end of her work on Volume Two, since when the indexing has been less provocative; she had settled the main problems and the pattern.

By now a rough notion of the probable division into volumes of these million words or more was possible. Volume One, it seemed, would extend from 1794 to Coleridge's departure from the Lakes in 1804 for Malta. The editorial notes were drafted, but there remained areas in which evidence had to be reconsidered, cross-references tidied up; various problems had either to be solved or declared insoluble. Peace and quiet and no telephone, no colleagues, no students, no domestic interruptions, and access to some university or good reference library were what I needed, and as at that time Canadian holders of Guggenheim awards were required to spend some months in the United States, I went first to a Vermont hillside not far from the University of Vermont, then later to that most beautiful old New England inn, the Sharon, in Sharon, Connecticut, alas no longer extant, then to the Berg Collection in New York.

Vermont brought me to a closer understanding of what Coleridge had to say about America and Americans. He was sympathetic to the Revolution and critical of the Government of England that had precipitated it. He learned a high regard for the American officers he met in Malta and Sicily, liking a certain crustiness (of which there is still a good deal in Vermont and Connecticut). He deplored anti-Americanism in England.

'I must say I cannot see much in Captain B. Hall's account of the Americans, but weaknesses,' he said, 'some of which make me like the Yankees all the better. How much more amiable is the American fidgettiness and anxiety about the opinion of other nations, and especially of the English, than the John Bullism, which affects to despise the sentiments of the rest of the world.'

But he thought 'it would be better for them if they were a trifle thicker-skinned'. That was in 1830.

It was from Vermont, while Coleridge was still alive, where the Rev. James Marsh was President in the eighteen twenties, that the transcendental haze taken to be Coleridge's philosophy was adopted by American transcendentalists. I had hoped to find out about the beginnings of that influence, through Marsh and such of his pupils as W.G.T.Shedd, the editor in 1847 of the first attempt at a collected edition of Coleridge. Shedd left his books to the Vermont University Library. Professor Julian Lindsay, kindness itself as my guide in Vermont, quoted with gusto and hilarious commentary an earlier Coleridgian there who perfectly represented the temper of those earnest, dogmatic times. The Reverend Aaron Pease in 1854 declaimed in ringing rhetorical tones 'the literary and philosophical creed of a Vermont alumnus':

'1 He believes in *Conscience* . . .
2 He believes in the distinction between the Reason and the Understanding . . .
3 He believes in the distinction between Nature & Spirit . . .
4 He believes in Coleridge . . .
5 He believes in Professor Marsh . . . for whenever one of these great names is pronounced the other is not a great way off . . .
6 He believes in the faculty of the University of Vermont . . .
7 He believes in the University of Vermont . . .
Finally . . . when another fifty years has passed away . . . the same doctrine will be held, and the same great men will be revered.'

It was the high point of my New England visit. Such speeches help one to understand a certain natural reaction against Coleridge, especially in the United States, and to realise the necessity of editing his actual words, which to our generation display more and more the inquirer, the observer of life at all levels, the asker of questions, rather than the stentorian deliverer of rigid creeds. But Coleridge has survived all his devotees, even Aaron Pease, and he will survive us.

From Vermont, January–February seemed a good time to go to the Huntington Library in Pasadena, a stretch under that unaltering boring blue sky, which somehow at that time represented the intellectual climate underneath it. This was greatly relieved by the presence of Sir George and Lady Clark from Oxford, and the Ed Bostetters from Seattle, all new acquaintances. Sir George Clark and I were the only persons in the Athenaeum Club who walked twice daily to the Huntington and back, so that I was treated to some very good talk, especially about British and European history and its pedagogy. Bostetter was the first person who at my elbow read the typescript of Volume One of the *Notebooks*, both Coleridge's text and my notes. Bos was a splendid enjoyer and appreciator, and witnessing his chuckles, astonishment, delight and squirming excitement was a great boost to the editorial morale.

By this time, though the Notes were in typescript, there were still holes that could be plugged only in the British Museum. And as I was not yet absolutely certain whether Volume One should include the Malta journey or not, it was decided by Bollingen, especially in view of the Guggenheim freedom I was enjoying, that I should go in March to England and thence to Malta, where Coleridge lived in 1804 and 1805.

Coleridge went to Malta in the spring of 1804 in search of health, in an effort to separate himself both from opium and from his torturing love for Sara Hutchinson. There he became private secretary to the British High Commissioner, Sir Alexander Ball, and in that capacity toured the island, conducted interviews and negotiations of every sort, and was generally active in the governing of Malta. He was in fact the administrator second in importance to Ball. Because he did so much writing of the official sort, and perhaps too because he was lonely and depressed, his notes on the life and landscape of Malta are not so full as they might otherwise have been, but they do touch on all sorts of unexpected matters. From Malta he returned home by way of Sicily (where he twice climbed Etna) and Italy; it was more than nine months of journeying and much solitary reflection between Naples, Rome, Florence, Pisa and Leghorn. It seemed necessary for me to try to decipher as much as possible of the text before leaving England and the manuscripts, but equally necessary to carry typescripts with me and try, by understanding them on the spot, to fill the gaps.

The wrestling in the Manuscripts Room went on every day, and most evenings another bit of wrestling, with Berlitz Italian. But not every evening. An English spring comes even to the brick and concrete of Bloomsbury, and it meant Sunday walks over heaths and commons. The evenings have left vivid recollections of literary encounters with Douglas Grant (busy on Hazlitt), John Hayward, editor of the *Book Collector*, and many others; Margaret Murray

I saw once in someone's digs, she who had set the world by the
ears in the nineteen-twenties with her *Witch Cult in Western
Europe*, a brilliant woman, now old and frail, sitting in a corner in
silence, 'the natural silence of old age'. To a young admirer of her
work, it was a salutary shock, a death's head suddenly come upon—
a great scholar her mortality all exposed. The whole of time was
not ahead of me after all! (Yet there was a twist in my exaggerated
sentiment. About ten years after this Margaret Murray wrote *My
First Hundred Years*!)

More happily memorable were some Sunday afternoon teas with
Walter de la Mare, 'WJ' to his friends. He was nearly eighty when
I first met him in 1952; unwell, and hypochondriacal, feeling
frailer than he looked. He had a bright eye that sometimes caught
yours sharply, rather like a wren's, but sometimes danced in merri-
ment, and sometimes looked sadly and darkly inwards. He loved
visitors, and non-academic literary talk. Not suffering fools gladly,
however, and I suspected, in order to choose his own conversation,
he had developed to a high degree of skill the art of asking strange
questions. He would talk about poetry, about the house he lived in,
about wondrous events like *seeing* a tree struck by lightning, about
witchcraft, any aspect of the invisible—dreams, memory—and all
sorts of thoughts connected with death.

I used to take him some of my Coleridge quotations for spotting.
Though he offered no solutions he talked enchantingly about
some of them, speculating wildly, producing shouts of laughter
from his guests to accompany his own quiet chuckling. (He was
proud of the fact that when he went to the Palace for his CH he
made the Queen laugh more heartily than royal etiquette usually
permits.)

He was not an ardent Coleridgian, but to prove to me that he had
early perceived in Coleridge a certain quality he regarded highly,
namely a respectful awareness of children and the child intelligence, he sent for a copy of his *Stuff and Nonsense* and read
aloud:

> 'My aged friend, Miss Wilkinson,
>   Whose mother was a Lambe,
> Saw Wordsworth once, and Coleridge, too,
>   One morning in her p'ram.
> . . .

> Birdlike the bards stooped over her—
>   Like fledglings in a nest;
> But Wordsworth said, "Thou harmless babe!"
>   And Coleridge was impressed.'

He had assumed that as a student of Coleridge I might be anti-Wordsworth, which led to an argument in which I defended Wordsworth, even for his treatment of Coleridge, and told him that my first real experience of poetry was *Tintern Abbey*.

'Yes,' he said, 'when you were a slightly soppy adolescent girl, I suppose [nail on head], but Wordsworth couldn't possibly *understand* Coleridge, could he? There are no *caves* in Wordsworth. Now Coleridge is full of caves, isn't he? You must be exploring them in the notebooks.

'Do you know,' he said, 'a girl of ten read *Kubla Khan* to me the other day. I wish you could have heard her. You would then have a clearer grasp of that poem. Children understand things, you know, that adults have forgotten.'

'As Wordsworth pointed out,' I had to remind him, for he loved a *touché*.

Speaking on one occasion of the wonderful glosses on *The Ancient Mariner*, he suddenly asked me if I had ever heard anyone unconsciously speak verse.

'Yes! An Irish cousin!' I said, for I recalled standing one glorious sunny morning in a hayfield high on the outskirts of Belfast, the larks singing overhead, the sweet new-mown hay around us, with the massed chimneys of a grim slum area belching smoke below, and Bob saying,

'How do they do it, Kathleen, how do they do it?
And they never having the sight of a green field!'

De la Mare's face glowed. 'Lovely!' he said. 'But of course I asked you that question because *I* wanted to tell *you* a story!' He had the smile of a naughty boy who has learned how to win his way to impunity.

'One night many years ago—just after the end of that first war—I used to come up out of the underground very late or in the early hours of the morning—I was working on a newspaper then—and regularly, where I came up, there was an old fellow with a sort of pup-tent sitting over a brazier, watchman over some works of some

kind, and I sometimes got into conversation with him. One particularly fine starry night he told me the sky reminded him of
Palestine, and of being there with an artillery unit during the war,
of the beauty of it, and how he loved it and all its Biblical associations, and he said, as if to cap all,

"And we watered our horses at the Pool of Siloam!"'

De la Mare beat out the metre with his finger. '*Si lo am, Si lo am*,
what a word!'

As he talked, bells began ever so faintly to tinkle at the back of
my mind. That week, looking at various volumes of his poems in
Bryce's bookshop in Museum Street I found *Winged Chariot*, and
on page eighteen a marginal gloss which read, 'And we watered our
horses at the Pool of Siloam'. On the next occasion of Sunday tea
in Twickenham, I reminded him of our conversation about glosses
and his quoting a line of unconscious verse. 'You know,' I said, 'I
found that in print the other day!' His face paled, so that I was
almost alarmed lest I had frightened him seriously—until I produced his volume from under my jacket, open at the page. There
was a burst of joy. Clutching my copy and running his fingers down
the pages he pointed out that some of his glosses were in quotation
marks, others not. The old night watchman's line was in quotes,
and a few others, but most were not.

'You see,' he said, 'I am an incorrigible reviser, and my son is
very patient with me and lets me have proof after proof, but finally
there comes a day when he says, "Now this *really* must be the
last." It often happens that at that point I have still a few precious
new lines that can't be left out—so—not being able to alter the
number of lines on the page-proofs, I stick 'em in the margin. I try
to be honest; if they are the words of other persons, they go in
quotation marks.'

April approached, and the struggle with readings in the seven
notebooks that survived Coleridge's Mediterranean journeys was
not over. Often in pencil, some of them stained by sea water or
rain, proper names mis-heard and mis-spelt and sometimes in-
comprehensible, some entries written in awkward postures or
scrawled in the hurry of travel—there was a limit to what could be
read without local knowledge. I must be off. Coleridge had written,

'Friday, April 6th, 1804—got on board the Speedwell, expecting to sail instantly / but the wind westerd again /

Saturday April 7th / quite calm / beautiful sight / Isle of Wight, & the Ships below it / and on the other side 9 men of war in zigzag semicircle, & in the interspace all sorts of smaller Ships, some with sails reefed, others all flying—the Sun on some, some in shade / their different Shapes & sizes & distinctnesses, & the Portsea Land &c a fine background, into which the sight dies away & is satisfied. The different Signals, Drums, Guns, Bells, & the sound of Voices weighing up & clearing Anchors. Wind all against us / . . .

Monday, April 9th, really set sail.'

On April 18th, Easter Sunday, a hundred and fifty years later, I followed, by aeroplane.

IX

1954

London was shining bright and clear, a still, sweet morning when I
left; Malta when I arrived was cold, wet, windy and miserable. It
felt the more so because I did not find a comfortable hotel. Having
had no familiarity with the concept 'travel expenses' I naively
interpreted it to mean transportation to and fro, with no notion
whatever of the inclusion of hotel bills, either abroad or in London.
Being still in the lower ranks when academic salaries at best were
not quite human, I found myself every day pinching pennies. So
it was a cheap and nasty hostel and what with chill marble floors
and general dampness in a late wet spring, including damp beds, I
caught a dreary cold.

But I was armed with S.T.Coleridge's notes, and agog to
compare his sight-seeing of a hundred and fifty years ago with
mine.

'Friday Afternoon, 4 °clock, April 18th, 1804,' (he wrote *April*
for *May*) 'the Speedwell dropt anchor in the Harbour of Malta—
one of the finest in the world / the Buildings surrounding it on all
sides, of a neat even new-looking Sand-free stone. Some unfinished . . . looked like Carthage when Æneas visited it / or a
burnt out place—. . . Found myself light as a blessed Ghost—'

It is part of the delight of trekking round after so close and arti-
culate an observer as Coleridge, that you see not only what your
own eyes tell you, but much that you might otherwise have missed;
such as the charm of lizards, the subject of a detailed entry; the
beauty of a prickly pear tree and of the 'conch-shaped' butterfly
flower; the conjunction of fortifications and orange-gardens, of
blossom and fruit on the trees together; or the 'sudden bellow shot
high up into the air with bomb-like burst' of a Maltese street vendor.
Moreover, the personality behind sensory responses like Coleridge's

relates him to the very stones, sometimes to send chills down the spine.

'. . . it is all height & depth—you can walk nowhere without having whispers of Suicide, toys of desperation . . .'
he told his pocket notebook.

'O Evening—when Loneliness is Dreariness—'. And he found the noises intolerable, from donkeys, cats, cocks, bells, 'In the inhabited Half of the Isle is it possible, in calm air, to be anywhere out of the Sound of Steeple Clock & Church Bells?' 'Day cries—Night-bellowings—Guns'.

Perhaps more important even than the clarification of some specific details, my Malta expedition conveyed vividly this intense loneliness on a small island—sixteen miles long—where Coleridge's only conversations were with military men or civil servants and one Italian newspaper editor. The English administration did not attempt to learn the language, nor did Coleridge; he found it a jumble mainly of Italian and Arabic, and as he was only beginning to learn Italian the mixture was daunting to one who considered himself but a bird of brief passage. The number and style of the priests ('most majestic peripheries of Paunch'), with whom he might have had much in common had they been more intellectual or more public-spirited, made him more intensely Protestant and anti-Roman Catholic for the rest of his life. In warm weather he suffered as an asthmatic from heat and humidity; in cold weather from bone-chilling damp buildings, all stone including the floors. It must have been for him a claustrophobic place without escapes or outlets. In the Napoleonic wartime, convoys bearing letters from home, or back again, were few and irregular. The sense of isolation amounting to rejection by life was all but intolerable. No wonder he talked to himself in his notebooks; for me the memoranda began to take on added meaning.

My week in Malta had its genial aspects, nevertheless. One of them was the attentiveness all week long of an archivist in the Royal Archives, Joseph Galea. Another was being conducted round the church of St John the Divine by Sir Hannibal Scicluna, who was writing a book on it, the church of the Knights of St John, of which order he was a member. He introduced me to a young teacher, Donald Sultana, very quiet, very courteous, but with a quite impenetrable façade. I should have liked to chat as to a colleague, but it was not possible. Shyness? Reservations of some kind? My wrong approach? I could not make out. He did not communicate to me his own interest in Coleridge.

I discussed with Sir Hannibal, and Sultana, and Galea, the possibility of there being S.T.Coleridge papers yet undiscovered in Malta. They thought not, though there had been rumours of city walls bombed in the war and official documents thus disgorged flying about the streets, later to be sold in the street bazaars or by hawkers. The men were much put out by a scholar who had written an identical letter to five persons, full of questions, involving time and searches. 'Did he think we all had that much time to waste, repeating each other's work?' they said. They had decided on a uniformly negative answer.

A few days later, however, Galea, in showing me the library and the archives, produced a bundle of proclamations printed over Coleridge's signature. STC as Secretary to the British High Commissioner may well have written some of them. These interesting and hitherto unknown documents I was able to have photographed and to include in an Appendix to the *Notebooks* Volume Two. It was entertaining to see Coleridge's authority attached to instructions to the Maltese to repair their waggon wheels, notices to army personnel about pay and discipline. There was one thoroughly Esteccean proclamation, of banishment to Gozo of a woman convicted of Jew-baiting, linked perhaps to his notebook entries agonizing over 'The persecution of the Jews' in May 1805. It presented an odd problem because there was not more than handful of Jews in Malta at that time. They had fled to Italy, mainly to Venice, when the Order of St John occupied the island from 1530 to 1798, and had not yet begun to return. Cecil Roth, whom I consulted, said positively there were none there in 1805, but Coleridge's notebooks showed otherwise.

Another unexpected fragment of Maltese history came out of an enquiry arising from a notebook entry. Coleridge, touring the island on horseback, with Sir Alexander Ball, recorded a 'sight just before Macluba [Magluba] of the fine Sea combe where Sir A. landed'. Galea was convinced Coleridge was in error; the sea could not be seen from that spot, and anyway tradition had it that Alexander Ball and his troops had landed elsewhere. On the last afternoon Galea took me by car to Magluba to prove his point.

Coleridge is not usually wrong in that sort of way, being normally precise visually, so I had to be persuaded. As we drew nearer the spot I could see Galea beginning to waver. There is a narrow tidal bay, a ravine with steep banks. When we examined them we could see a possible good landing for boats. From Coleridge's spot we could see his Devonshire combe—though not the sea itself. Everyone's honour was satisfied. One does not usually think of Coleridge as a source for a new insight into military history.

From Malta Coleridge went twice to Sicily, where I followed him. In Syracuse it was not hard to find his church with 'the little John Nobodies with chubby heads & wings looking up the Virgin's pettiskirts as roguishly as may be'. He contrasted 'the tawdry modern Front', as well he might, with the fluted Doric columns of the old Greek temple of Minerva—so clean and simple—on which the heavy, ugly church had been superimposed. Syracuse was a lovely time—with a trip by local bus (and all sorts of shouted local instructions) to the Greek theatre, to Targia and, above all for beauty, to Timoleon's Euryalus, with its glorious view over both harbours of Syracuse and great sweeps of countryside. Coleridge wrote of them all. The old guide at Euryalus could hardly hobble over the ancient fortress of Dionysius, the fifth-century Tyrant of Syracuse, but he did, answering all my questions, finally becoming so involved that he demanded to see STC's notes and went through them avidly with me.

The next stop was Catania in the morning by train. Having by now learned that everything ceases in Sicily between noon and three, I made pell mell for the University and the English department, to ask for advice. I needed, for my own trip, information on Etna routes, and also some guidance as to Coleridge's probable route on his ascent; and I was in pursuit of a poem in Latin, which seemed to be connected with a monastery he visited somewhere in the neighbourhood. In the end, after many fruitless conversations, I had help from Professor Frosini of the School of Law, who made himself a most gracious host, escorted me about Catania, and introduced me to Sicilian ice cream. He was impressive, had read Coleridge's *Church and State* when doing his Oxford degree, had written a paper on T.S.Eliot which Eliot liked. He regarded Eliot as an important bridge between Protestant England and Roman Catholic Europe.

Frosini also took me to the learned Professoressa Naselli (I hope
after all these years I have her name correctly spelled), who went
over all Coleridge's Etna notes with me. The Latin poem, she
agreed, probably had to do with the monastery of S. Niccolo del
'Arena, secularized in 1870, when the records were seized; they
might now be in the local archives. The poem might have been on
a tablet or in a visitors' album and guest book. The monastery
itself, now a school, was well worth the visit for the view from the
tower (130 steps) and for the little old guide, full of fun and no
English, who took me up.

I made next day for the archives and had some difficulty in
finding the building. There seemed to be no distinguishing features,
but if you just *look* hard enough in Sicily, for anything, a head is
sure to pop out of an upper window and shout, 'What's the matter?'
You grow accustomed to the feeling that you have been under
observation for some time, probably looking half-witted, because
in the end after a good deal of gesticulation, shouting, laughter,
consultation of someone within and every passer-by without, you
are set on your course. But the archives yielded nothing.

The Professoressa had confirmed my suppositions from Coleridge's notes that there were two ascents of Etna, and that at least
one was from the Catania side through Nicolosi. There was a great
referring to old maps and guide books, she being an authority on
travellers to Sicily. Every time any unsuspecting colleague poked a
head through her door he was sent off to look for another map or
reference book. I couldn't have had better advice.

The bus for the *Rifugio*, last stop part-way up Etna, left at seven
in the morning. From over-optimism, geographical ignorance, and
inadequate Italian, I had the impression it would be possible to
ascend to the crater that day; as it proved, I had the rest of the day
to bask in the sun and breathe that glorious heady mountain air.
The mountain-side fairly pulls one out to walk on it. After four or
five miles I returned to the *Rifugio* to find the whole family sitting
on the open porch, legs over the side—a wonderful row of sunny
Sicilian faces all breaking into smiles. I sat down too, and demanded
tea, *con limone*. It came, and a deck chair, and some conversation
about how *molto bello* it all was. I looked forward to a couple of
hours before dinner in which to catch up my notes and some
correspondence, but a young man who had earlier fitted me with

climbing shoes proffered an invitation to one of the nearby craters.
Molto bello, etc, etc. I said I was a bit tired, needed rest, and so on,
but he pleaded. It was not clear to me whether he was to be a guide
for a price, or whether this was just ardent hospitality, or something
else again. Naturally I had been warned about the attentions of
Sicilian men.

Had I not read Emily Lowe on *Unprotected Females in Sicily,
Calabria, and on the top of Mount Aetna*? In 1859 she described
how she and her unwilling mother had ascended Etna, dropping
off 'shawls' and 'heavy petticoats' every hundred yards or so, and
how, after a few agreeable storm-stayed days of flirtation in a
Benedictine monastery on the mountain, she could give the assurance that 'no young ladies need in future take the trouble of the
experiment'. So the doorstep conversation at the *Rifugio* went on—I
was not supposed to understand—to the effect that the lad might as
well give up, no English ladies would go unaccompanied. By this
time I was curious to see what he seemed genuinely eager to show,
and there was perhaps a point in trying out the boots. Perhaps I
was just following Emily Lowe. In any case, off we went, round an
old crater, down the outside of it, running and sliding on the
crumbly, iron-grey, iron-brown lava.

It was lovely, a bit like skiing, and except that the panorama was
largely bathed in mist, through which I was expected to see that it
would be *molto bello* if only we could see it, and that I grew weary of
having to make grateful exclamations to this effect, it was entertaining. The boy alleged he was a poet, washing dishes at the
Rifugio for his keep because he loved this landscape, trying in vain
to get his poems published. He recited a lot—of his own?—some
of them about Etna. Certainly as he pointed to the sharp changes in
colour and contour with the movement of light on them, I began to
feel that this weird purplish world (near sunset) could cast a spell
on me. As in Catania it was the experience of a landscape quickened
and extended through the sensibilities of one at home in it—whatever his motives.

There were many stops—to empty the lava from my too-large
boots, and to observe the subtler beauties of this abstract-seeming
scenery, and of course to struggle to talk. He had no word of
English. He asked me what I did. And when I told him, *scrivo, ma
non poeta* and was trying to explain that a famous English poet in

1805 had climbed Etna and that I was trying to understand his notes, a great light crossed his face. 'Ah—*lei è professoressa?*' At which he dropped on one knee, took my left hand and kissed it three times ceremoniously uttering some ritualistic form of words which though unintelligible to me made themselves sufficiently understood. From then on my boots had to be emptied more often, each time being unlaced and relaced with great flourishes to *la professoressa*. What was my age? I suggested he should guess.

'Thirty-four.'

'No,' I said, 'much older.' He subjected my face to detailed examination. 'No,' he said sternly, 'not more.' I told him I was nearly old enough to be his mother. I must be lying. He counted my wrinkles. 'Not possibly more than thirty-four.' Anyhow, whatever it was in years, he said, my real age was thirty-four. *Poeticé*, I suppose. He said he was twenty-eight. Perhaps I did not understand Italian numerals? He would teach me. '*Uno, due,*' etc. His face was a study—kindergarten teacher to a *professoressa*! One little pig went to market, etc., on the fingers. As we descended towards the *Rifugio*, stars coming out overhead and starry-lights below from some village, he said,

'You could marry me, and I could come to Canada with you. Will you?'

'And what would we live on?' Vulgar Canadian practicality raised the question.

'On my poems of course.'

'Printed in Italian?'

'Of course, what else?' He pouted like a child. I was lying again, not giving him the real reason why I wouldn't pay his fare to Canada. There was nothing in the least tiresome about it all, just a child-like game. Next day, he was all sun and smiles.

The ascent of Etna itself at four next morning was disappointing. We reached the crater but were not allowed to go round it because it was difficult to stand and push against the wind. As I learned from the Taormina paper next day, there was a real gale blowing in the whole area. We therefore sniffed the sulphurous smells, but so loud was the wind that we missed the famous artillery and thunder, and could see little of the panorama.

It was an exhilarating climb though, for a complete novice, and I was glad not to have missed it whatever the weather. Besides, what other bluestocking could boast of a proposal of marriage on the slopes of Etna?

The rest of the trip had its numerous beauties and also its painful or amusing moments. Such as Taormina, dripping everywhere with bougainvillia. Coleridge had written:

'Taormina, gray roofs & white fronts on its breast / Savage scenery, of various, leaping Outline, & *cut-glass* Surface / and the Clouds, & the Crater of Etna rising above.'

'The view of the Path from Taormina to the Theatre, & from the Theatre itself, surpasses all I have ever seen,' I read out from the typescript of his notes to a conversational Danish painter who offered me half an apple. While we were looking down into the theatre it suddenly came alive with perhaps 150 schoolgirls bright in royal-blue blazers, a priest directing them to take up positions illustrating how the theatre worked; an enchanting ballet-like moment with the priest the leading ballerina. 'Much more beautiful fifty years ago,' the painter said, 'and even more so in Coleridge's day, but it would be difficult to spoil it.'

A problem I wished to solve was Coleridge's route from Taormina to Messina, which by mere maps did not look reasonable. He wrote while at Giardini on the coastal road and then about nine or ten miles further on began to describe what could not be seen from that road. With the help of the hotel houseboy who accompanied me, it became clear that from Giardini he had taken a carriage up a steep road to a point where the carriage got stuck and then he made the rest of the climb to Castelmola on foot. We softies drove up, and saw the magnificent sweep of sea and mountainous hills Coleridge had struggled to describe. Coming down we met an old countryman having trouble with a mule. He was angry and the donkey stubborn. As we passed I gather he offered a coarse jibe to the effect that May was the mating month for these donkeys and they always behaved like fools then. The houseboy answered, 'Remember you were young once yourself, old man. Don't be too hard on the beast.' Or such was his delicate explanation to me of their exchange in dialect.

Malta is relatively flat and panoramically dull; Sicily was a first experience of a true Mediterranean lanscape. There was dire poverty everywhere, yet a relaxed sunniness, always time to play with children, poor children much better dressed than their parents. Talk is important, and conversation a drama not to be considered second to anything else. One stops dead in the street, face to face to have one's talk out, insouciantly blocking, quite suddenly sometimes, whoever might be coming up behind. There is no revulsion, as among the English, at bumping bodily or being bumped. Nothing seems to be too serious for too long; though a quarrel may be sudden, hot, even violent, it usually stops just as quickly. Tomorrow, who knows? Etna is always an uncertainty—a seductive one, the very name lovingly prolonged with an extra syllable in the middle of it—Etena. 'She' is so beautiful—so bountiful—is the lava not rich for grapes and olives?—and she is mysterious, changeable, deadly when she strikes. Kindliness costs nothing —and where life is hard it is better to smile and be friendly—tomorrow may bring another disaster—but in the meantime, the day is warm, and one may enjoy the opportunity to talk with a stranger. Time and history may be very long. Sicily reminded me of much in Ireland that against all commonsense and reason one loves to experience as a visitor.

After Sicily Coleridge took me to Naples, Rome, Florence, Pisa, and Leghorn, and on a few other jaunts he did not mention—to Pompeii for instance. Although he might have been expected to go, possibly he did not, for in 1805 Pompeii had been very little excavated. If he went, surely his inevitable meditations on life and death went into a notebook. (Some notebooks have been lost, probably at least three or four.) He was an excellent if unconventional guide. In Rome he pushed me into the cloisters of the *Trinità de' Monti* (special and grudging permission required) to see the crumbling, faded, begrimed S. Paolo frescoes (which he found disgusting and blasphemous). He led me to examine with his own exact attention Michelangelo's ceiling of the Sistine Chapel:' Take as an instance of the true Ideal Michel Angelo's despairing Woman at the bottom of the Last Judgment.' I followed him to the Café Greco where he used to meet Washington Allston, the painter who become a close friend, and other Americans; to the falls of Terni where he had climbed to the top, up the side of the face. My Italian taxi driver, his eyes filled with horror, assured me that no one ever did it now and that there was barbed wire at the top. But I had no need to follow the very footprints, for in the depleted state of the waterfall (from modern power developments there) I could see the original watercourse as Coleridge had described it; the text had not been clear to me before. In Florence the Uffizi was made the more interesting by the search for pictures to which he referred; and likewise Pisa, 'a grand and wild mass, especially by moonlight . . .' but what moved him, he said, 'with a deeper interest were the two Hospitals, one for men, one for women, the breadth & the height of the rooms, the number largeness & good contrivance of the windows, the perfect cleanliness & good order—what forms their strict peculiarity, the great door of open iron work . . .'

An expedition of Olevano Romano was especially glorious one perfect May day. Coleridge in Rome in January 1806 was warned by a papal emissary that he was on Napoleon's blacklist for anti-French paragraphs he had written in the *Morning Post* a few years before and would not be safe when, as was expected daily, Napoleon rolled down upon Rome. This was Coleridge's story, often questioned or discounted, which correspondence has now come to light to confirm. It is a measure of the range of guns and of the size of troop movements in those times that he took refuge thirty miles away up in the hills of Olevano Romano in the house of Washington Allston. His description of the scene from Allston's garden made me eager to see it, and again one needed what help the physical features would lend to read the pencilled notes accurately. So, having booked seats for the first night of *Christoforo Colombo* at the Opera House for that evening, and feeling a little like a Christoforessa Columbina myself after following all sorts of wrong directions to the bus station, I just caught a local bus by a hairsbreadth. It was full of villagers going to San Vito, all very inquisitive, and friendly even when they found out I was a Canadian. (I was aware that Canadian artillery had pounded that valley not many years before.) The journey grew more beautiful by the mile. I had asked the driver to put me down at Olevano, but I need not have done so; it was decidedly the end of the line, and besides I should have recognized it from Coleridge's description:

'. . . The vale itself is diversified with a multitude of Rises, from Hillocks to Hills, and the Eastern Side of the circular mountain

Boundary vaults down into the vale in Leaps, forming Steps.—
The first Hills sink to rise into higher Hills that sink to rise into a
yet higher and the mountain boundary itself is the fifth Step.—
On the third Step, which is broad and heaves in many Hillocks,
some bare & like Cairns, some green, stands Olevano, its old
ruinous Castle with church-like Tower cresting the height of
this third Step / the town runs—down the Ridge in one narrow
Line almost like a Torrent of Houses; and where the last House
ends, more than half of the whole ridge, a narrow back of bare
jagged grey rock commences, looking like the ruins of a Town / a
green field finishes the ridge, which passes into the vale by a
Copse of young Oaks / on different heights on other Steps or other
Hills the towns of Civitella, Pagliano, Avita, Santo Spirito stick
like Eagle-nests, or seem as if the rock had chrystallized into
those forms / but how shall I describe the beauty of the roads,
winding up the different Hills, now lost & now re-appearing in
different arcs & segments of Circles . . .'

At the Bar-Ristorante de Valeri at the bus stop I ought to have
had lunch, but I hoped there might be another café at the top and
was drawn anyhow to follow those streets of stairs to the top,
cobbled and hard to walk on, growing narrower and more difficult,
some steps just carved out of rock. There were doorsteps at each
turn and a man mending shoes, a woman knitting, a girl reading a
pulp magazine, children in and out, everywhere. The higher one
got the more one felt a trespasser on private property; *'Buon giorno'*
was automatic, as natural as a greeting on a Canadian country
road. It was electric—a button pushed—closed or suspicious faces
opened wide, with and without teeth. No, nothing at the top, all
chiudo, they said, yet there was considerable conversation and
debate on the best advice as to how I might get in to see the old
ruin up there. A little boy led me on a ledge round the face of a
precipice (he carrying my handbag) but that path too ended in a
closed gate. However, from there he pointed to a painter's house,
now also *chiudo*. But he knew another one, maybe that was the one
I wanted—another painter—may be Americano. I gave him a few
lire and told him to meet me at the Ristorante after lunch.
The delightful woman in the Ristorante spoke an Italian totally
lost on me, and when we failed to understand each other over the

menu, they led me, in what was my first experience of the Mediterranean style, into the kitchen. Yes, I could have an omelette and
some cheese and good, *molto bello*, red wine. As I enjoyed it,
especially the truly memorable red wine, I became aware of two
black heads, four black eyes and two sets of very white teeth
grinning at the door. Hands waved. I waved. My twelve-year-old
guides. They waited, communicating their intentions for the afternoon to about a dozen, doubtless rival guides, all about the same
age, all lying on their stomachs facing downhill and waving their
arms about over that magnificent prospect. We set out finally on a
lovely road via S Antonio; not, I felt, the right direction, but I was
in their hands. They were trying hard for me, and the road was
breathtakingly varied and fine. The house turned out to have
belonged to a German artist until recent years, and again my defi-
ciency in the tenses of Italian verbs had probably led to a mistaken
interpretation. I could hardly care, the sun was warm and the day
perfect, the company enchanting. Suddenly I sniffed something
fragrant—the boys looked—I looked—honeysuckle in a hedge.
What was its name in Italian? Just as the boy, my first little friend,
picking a piece for me, looked up to say '*fiore del cuccu*' (cuckoo
flower) we all heard the call of a cuckoo! They looked as if one of us
had passed a miracle. That beautiful young face took on an
expression of absolutely blissful joy. It was a moment of some kind
of experience in common, mutually and perfectly recognized without
words. They then asked for cigarettes. For themselves? For their
elders? No. To sell—cigarettes being then prohibitively expensive
in Italy. I gave them one cigarette each and a few more lire and off
they went.

Something began to drift into my recollection of someone's
having said that Allston's house had become an Albergo. So I
called in at the Albergo di Roma and was ushered upstairs to see the
family photograph albums, by way of demonstration that this hotel
had been in the hands of this family for at least four generations;
but not quite back to 1806. The landlady was disappointed in her
inability to go back so far, but she was still of the firm and slightly
barbed opinion that this respectable house had never been inhabited by an American. Still, the inquiry gave me a glimpse of a
dark roomful of dark men, sitting over the remains of a late lunch,
talking about music and periodically one or other bursting into

song to illustrate a point. The naturalness and ease of it set a mood for the rest of the day.

The landlady pointed out to me another house which she thought might be the one I was looking for, now occupied by the priest, who however was not at home. Certainly it commanded some of the view Coleridge described. The visit there produced a good deal of verbose mirth. Well, of course I could look at the view; wasn't *looking* free? Did I not wish to see the inside of the house? Would I come next day when the priest would show me? The housekeeper led me down paths to two or three promontories where the panorama was too dramatic, too vast, too vivid in detail, to grasp, but as Coleridge had described it, especially in texture. Though buxom, my guide was very graceful, picked me some irises growing in the unweeded garden, warned me to beware of the donkey's hind legs, and intimated where I should stay if I were spending the night in Olevano—at the Albergo Tulli, not di Roma. Tulli would be cheaper and better. As I passed the door of Albergo Tulli I wished I were staying there and vowed to go back to that splendid landscape, where the villages perch, as Coleridge said, like eagles' nests, and where the *vino* (Coleridge twice noted it down)—*Vino rossi di Affile* (Affile is only a few miles from Olevano)—is superb. Though I had not succeeded entirely in what I thought was the aim of that journey, I certainly understood Coleridge's rapturous memoranda there much better.

Nobody prepared me for the noise of Florence, full of motorcycles, buses, trolleys, cars, all being driven at a furious pace and perpetually either screeching to a full stop or blasting away on their horns in all keys, sometimes crashing together at intersections, with volleys of angry shouting. My first impression was distasteful—noise, crowds, a kind of tourist-created squalor, advertisements cluttering the piazzas surrounded by palaces, a general sense of grandeur decayed, all a great shock to foretastes of Florence derived largely from the English poets.

I did not fail to call on them in the English Cemetery, where it was a pleasure to see that the paths to their graves were well-worn. Someone had put a red rose on Landor's stone. The morning was hot and sunny, one for a good pokey time in the tall grass, among the roses, and rhododendrons and cypress trees, and sweet little periwinkle here and there. The first name my eye lit upon provided

me with an answer to an unsolved notebook problem. Who was
Trajano Wallis, a child Coleridge knew in Naples, Rome or
Florence? Here was a stone, to George Augustus Wallis, erected by
his son Trajan, in memory of one noted for his skill and 'science'
in painting, an Englishman, from Surrey. I daresay I should
eventually have found the father anyhow, for he was a fairly well-
known painter and teacher, but the son? This was early days in my
searchings—one of those surprise gifts that beautifully simplified
things.

Italy was even harder to leave in the flesh than it is in the telling,
but I left it for Göttingen and a brief visit there with my dear old
friend and hostess of Allensteiner Schloss, Frau Irma von Ruperti.
We had corresponded even into the war years (she sent letters out
by people going to Switzerland or Sweden) and though guns
divided us, we had never really felt out of touch. Each year of the
war she had lost one relative, including her two sons, her husband
and her son-in-law, and there were no male members of the family
connexion left. So it was in some ways a harrowing meeting. Yet
the great thing was the instantaneous reunion; without a split
second of hesitation or awkwardness we were back where we had
always been with each other. My German was in fact more fluent,
not because I had been speaking any, but chiefly because the
Italians had loosened my stiff, inhibited, Canadian tongue.

From Frankfurt by air to England, the may in bloom, pink and
white, greenness everywhere, and all those nostalgia-making
English smells. London and home again, for so it always feels. It
was on this return, with no hotel booked, I found the St Margaret's,
three minutes from the British Museum, run by a charming family
from Tuscany named Marazzi. Simple, clean, and above all an
obliging management who gave me a largish room on the back four
flights up, and put into it a large work table and an extra reading
lamp and a vase or two for my flowers. For several summers this
was to be my room; a good deal of proof-reading was done there
after BM hours (in those days the BM always closed at five), against
the competition of snatches of Italian operatic arias coming up the
stairs from housemaids and kitchen help.

There were some other wonderful breaks in that 1954 summer.
There was a week-end in July at Stonegrave with the Herbert
Reads, when he drove me in pelting rain over his beloved Yorkshire,

through the Sara Hutchinson country to Gallow Hill (and then was too shy to knock on the door), and to the village of his childhood and the dripping green churchyard where, pointing to the family plot he said, 'There is where I shall lie one day.' And where indeed he lies now, 'Herbert Read 1896–1968, Knight, Poet, Anarchist.' The week-end was a painful one, for I had just shortly before had the news, which I stupidly did not disclose, of my father's sudden death; but our friendship survived what must have been for him a grim and dim week-end.

July brought another visit to Ottery. The fête was to be held on the nineteenth and again I was invited to help with tours of the house—of course with many uncomplimentary remarks from Himself on my conduct last time. But it was again a touching visit, and, as it proved, the last in his lifetime.

Ottery was now a place for a good rest among delicious familiar sights and smells and sounds; the church bells, the Ottery cocks, the hard Devon shoes on the hard cobbled hill, and for being with my two dear Frumps. It was no longer a place for work. In those years on the return from Ottery to London one of my little jobs for him was to go to Buckingham Palace 'to sign the book'. As a peer of the realm, he and his lady were invited to the Royal garden party, but he was something of a recluse, hated the journey to London and all the bustle and dislocation of his quiet days that it involved. If a guest does not sign the book himself he must send a deputy to do so. Hence my visits to Buckingham Palace.

Back in London, the last weeks of that summer were particularly hectic in the British Museum, but not so panicky as to eliminate London's joys.

There was a good hour one day when Jack Barrett came to the British Museum to see the notebooks, the full array of the fifty-six now in the Department of Manuscripts. It was a delight to me to see Jack trembling with excitement as he handled them, not just with respect but with tenderness, lightly, carefully, his face flushing and words failing him at the sense of intimacy these objects conveyed, and also at the difficulty, to an unaccustomed eye, in reading them. Lovely to have a publisher so unhardened to the rigours of the work behind books!

Helen Darbishire, that summer, took me into her confidence in some Dove Cottage matters, and was most generous in worrying through some of my Coleridge problems. *The Letters of Sara Hutchinson* were to come out in September, and Joanna and I had a pre-publication celebration with a grand lunch and a matinée performance of *A Day By the Sea* with Sybil Thorndike, John Gielgud, Ralph Richardson and Irene Worth. The British Museum was full of people working on Coleridge—John Colmer from Khartoum, John Beer, George Whalley, Mary Wilkinson on Coleridge's Germans, Mohammed Badawi from Egypt on Coleridge's Shakespearian criticism, and several others more peripherally. Life was strenuous with talk, so much so that someone proposed we choose a pub to which we would make our ways when we were not tired of other Coleridgians and of talking shop. Generally we seemed to be avid for exchanges, and for a few years the Crown in New Oxford Street became the Coleridge pub.

This was the summer of reading the galleys of Volume I of the *Notebooks*, a fascinating if alarming business which was greatly assisted by the devotion and wit and clear reading voice of Oliver Stonor. What at this point made me decide to have one more look at Notebook 22 I do not know, but it precipitated the kind of crisis every editor of new material dreads. This arose out of the plan to present the material chronologically.

It should be explained that we thought of five volumes, each in two parts, (1) Coleridge's memoranda and (2) my notes. Roughly sketched out we thought the divisions would be—

Volume 1. 1794–January 1804. The moment of departure from the Lakes or London for Malta seemed a natural break.

Volume 2. 1804–1808. The Malta journey, the return to England and the Lakes, up to another departure for London to give the first of his literary lectures.

Volume 3. 1808–1819. From the beginning of the first lecture series to the end of the last series—material much intertwined.

Volume 4. 1819–1827. A crisis in health and a return to the Church of England, years of strenuous scientific reading, and of the publication of his most popular work in his lifetime, *Aids to Reflection*.

Volume 5. 1827 to the end. Largely theological, with some charming personal entries.

Notebook 22 was not within the plan for Volume I, having long ago been deemed of a date later than January 1804. The first date physically appearing in it, recorded by Coleridge, was December 1804. That should put it in Volume 2. But N 22 was difficult to date with assurance, being really a composite of several notebooks inserted one into the other. I suppose it had always subliminally left me a nagging worry about its chronology. On returning to it I suddenly saw that the handwriting in the early pages—clearly not STC's—was that of Sara Hutchinson; work on her letters had made that hand familiar to me. Until that moment it had seemed that these first entries were Malta ones; written by Sara, they must have been written *before* STC's departure, and must therefore be included in Volume 1. Here was a nice kettle of fish. The serializing was completed, and to alter it would be to throw out cross-references in the hundreds of notes, as well as to shift all the numeration of the text from that point on. The re-dating of Sara's entry also meant the re-dating and inclusion of eighteen others from the same notebook. The physical problem of including them could be solved by inserting them with alphabetical designations added to the previous number. But there was a more serious problem. The first leaves had been lost—no cover on this notebook—and so Sara's transcript, more than six pages of dull, colourless Latin, had no beginning. It was not classical Latin; whose was it? There were no idiosyncratic identifying words, the only proper names were Socrates and Plato, Hector and Achilles, too common to be helpful clues. And not only this first entry in the book but the whole little additional clutch of eighteen entries also introduced problems of source-hunting.

One pores over such a passage, hoping for hunches. It was all about association and memory, a subject discussed at length by scores of mediaeval monks. Memory after all was a function of the soul. Half by deduction, half by recollection, I remembered what I ought to have thought of at once, Coleridge's reference in *Biographia* to Aquinas on Aristotle's *Parva Naturalia*, specifically the essay on memory and reminiscence. Something else clicked. In 1949 I had, en route for Scotland, visited Durham Cathedral Library and examined the borrowers' book to see what Coleridge had read there in 1801. One of his borrowings was the second volume of the works of Aquinas in the eighteen-volume Antwerp edition of 1612.

Was his commentary on that essay of Aristotle in that volume? There was no copy of that edition in the British Museum. Time was short but a dash to Oxford brought the answer. The essay was indeed in Volume 2, and the peculiar printing of that edition explained certain oddities in Sara's transcript of the passage. Thus it became possible to date the entry within a month, 25 July–24 August 1801, the period when Coleridge had the folio from the Durham Cathedral library, when he and Sara were both staying at her brother's farm at Bishop's Middleham where she copied it out. With this solution of source and date, other entries in the group also fell into place. Somehow the few days before sailing for home had a way of becoming crisis-prone.

By the end of August I was dreaming of some peaceful days on Georgian Bay, and by the tenth of September I was there, living in the canoe, swimming four times a day, finding the same toe-holds on the rocks, the same peaceful grooves of companionship, the usual visits from Ojibway friends. After a week Jessie went back to her job and I was alone on the island.

These days were recovery—getting sleep—not having to meet a single person, no obligations, no need to look at a clock. No deadlines. But more positive too.

I went out for a paddle under the night sky. It was a black night, no moon, but full of stars bright enough to make the pines heavy and dark—the great Dipper very near—Orion unusually bright— the canoe slid over the reflections, for the water was still as only a large body of water can be still. Out on the reefs something could be heard lashing up. Johnson had agreed that morning when I said we would surely have a blow. 'Yes,' he said, 'we have eastwind two days now. It will blow.'

The universe seemed at once larger and more intimate here than anywhere on my travels. In no other place is it such a satisfaction— just to *be*, just to exist, to be a part of it, related to it by living into it.

I found in England I was unreasonably irritated sometimes at being introduced as the editor of the Coleridge notebooks, or worse, as 'the authority on Coleridge', a ridiculous expression. Why the annoyance? I suppose one resists the pressure it represents, especially when work is at a strenuous stage. One resists it also because, the truth is, editing Coleridge requires dozens of people.

No single person is an authority on him; also, being identified
wholly with only a part of one's work however enjoyable, can be
irritating. Anyhow, I was glad to get back with old friends—like
Johnson Tabobandung who knew nothing of all that and was glad
to see me all the same.

Johnson in his boat arrived one day from the opposite direction
as I was paddling in with a canoe full of roots for the fireplace. He
greeted me at the shore, our first meeting of the season, shook my
hand, delivered a note, and said, 'I unload canoe. I think you have
to write answer.' Practical, no fuss, no unnecessary explanations.
I did as I was told and then we settled down and caught up on the
family news—Russell, up north somewhere; Barbara in the sana-
torium getting better, reading a lot; Arnold talking of getting
married *maybe*; Hubert, big boy, working; Johnny the youngest,
tallest of all now. He hopes all the boys going to work together this
winter—sending logs to the pulp factory. Mrs Tabobandung?
Oh, she is fine, works too hard, like all women. Suddenly he
asked, 'Are you fifty?' I complained that he was rushing me ahead
a little and not so polite as men in Sicily. 'How that?' So I told him
about little Giacomo on the slopes of Etna. Johnson kept murmuring,

'All those strange places you go to! Where is Malta?—you sent
me postcard from there.' I told him about how the Maltese had to
gather stones into walls to find and hold soil, and about them
growing grapes and oranges and other fruit—till finally it struck
me to say—'You must know, Johnson, about Malta! You preach
sometimes; that's where St Paul got shipwrecked.'

'Ohhh,——yes! I read about that in *Life* Magazine!' Then the
room rocked with his great belly laughter, for incongruity is the
essence of Indian humour. He was eager to hear more, full of
questions, so I told him about Pompeii, buried nearly two thousand
years ago in lava, about the houses and streets, the dog petrified in
mid-howl, the mummified human figures trying to run away, the
bread found in the oven. Johnson was all eyes and ears.

'But it's good to be back—here, in this place.' I said.

'Where it's quiet,' he said, nodding.

We strolled down to the dock. 'I certainly glad to see you safe
home. All those strange places you go to, all those people. Did you
speak to them in *their* language?'

'Not very well,' I said, thinking truthfully of my struggles, 'but some. You see I had to find out things. For my work.' He shook his head. 'Never know who you talking to over there. That a very dangerous thing you do—speaking to them in *their* language.'

I defended my folly. 'They're not really very different from us,' I said, 'when you know them a little. And anyhow, some people think I am doing a far more dangerous thing staying up here all by myself on this island, now the summer's over.'

He looked utterly astonished.

'What could happen to you here? Everybody gone home!' And after a second there came again an explosion of laughter as he himself appreciated what he had said. He went off chuckling. Only man is vile; and neither travel nor book-learning will teach anyone for sure when it's going to blow.

I suggested a cord of wood would be acceptable. He was not sure. Maybe to-morrow. Maybe next day. It came, and in due course was unloaded and neatly piled. After a smoke and another little chat, well, they'd 'better move. Wind has swung round to south.' 'Yes,' I said, 'but you said there would be a big blow.'

'No, I didn't say. You said it,' he came back.

'But you *agreed* with me.'

He began to laugh—'Well, I couldn't disagree with a lady like you that's been all over the world, could I?'

X

1955-1959

Early in February 1955, when the news of the Canadian acquisition of a Coleridge collection by Victoria College reached the English press, Humphry House wrote another angry letter, this time not to me but to *The Times*, asking by whose authority the manuscript of *Christabel* and other national treasures had silently left the country. It was a good letter as far as it went, and with others that followed had some useful far-reaching effects in Britain in emphasizing the need for caution in the dispersal of manuscripts. John Hayward and others joined in the fray. Though I agreed with them in part— for the secrecy imposed on me had been an uncongenial element in the transaction—I felt nevertheless that as one who had had a part in obtaining the Coleridge collection for the British Museum a few years before, and now the smaller one for Toronto, I must reply with the case for the defence.

I pointed out that Coleridge manuscripts were already widely dispersed, that the British Museum had been given the first refusal of what we had acquired, and that a distinction should be made between the scattering by auction of valuable manuscript materials into private hands and their preservation in a university library. Far more serious blows to Coleridge studies in recent years were two sales of Coleridgeana in Oxford in the 1940s at prices prohibitive to most scholars. I argued that Canadian students would benefit in their studies by seeing a few real manuscripts. We did not propose any restricted use. We hoped, in becoming custodians of this collection, to share as hosts in that interchange of scholars which we who usually did the Atlantic crossing knew to be highly rewarding. The reversal of the direction of the crossing would, we hoped, not minimize the rewards, certainly not to us. And for good measure I enlisted Coleridge, himself who in his day envisaged the importance to civilization of the cultural unity of the English-speaking world. If this could not be achieved in scholarship in the humanities, what hope was there for us?

My letter was dated, Toronto, February 8th 1955; Humphry died suddenly of a heart attack on February 14th. I doubt if he saw my letter; at any rate, we did not resolve this difference between us as we had the earlier one. He was not always fair to me, nor did we much like each other personally, but his death was, for me as editor of the notebooks, a loss I still feel.

In March at Ottery St Mary Geoffrey Coleridge died, also of a heart attack. He was a friend who had always shown his better side to me. Here were the first breaks in the circle of those of us who were trying to give to the public the possibility of knowing the Coleridge who had poured himself out in hundreds of manuscripts still unknown. Lady Coleridge, shattered and lonely as her letters revealed her, but maintaining the stiff upper lip, immediately left the Chanter's House for a little hotel in Cornwall, where her half-blind sister was in need of her.

At Easter of this year the first corrected galleys of Volume 1 of the Notebooks went off to Bollingen in New York. The Foreword and Introduction, if I remember correctly, were still to be re-written for the last time, with some other parts of the front and back matter. The summer on Georgian Bay was full of all this, and of joyful encounters with the fresh materials of Volume 2. In order to establish securely the limits of the first volume, a good deal of work had already been done on entries of uncertain date, many of which were assigned eventually to the second or even later volumes. So the text of Volume 2 was not unknown to me, but most of it was still to be worked on. The stage when one first sets out really to explore new material, really to wrestle with it, is the most ex-hilarating moment of the whole editorial operation. Each new volume presents new problems and, with Coleridge, big additions to the mental terrain.

My typescript of Volume 1 had gone in to Bollingen, Text and Notes, by the fall of 1953. Problems of printer, design, discussions about style, and the copy-editing in New York consumed 1954. The whole of 1955 was lived in a recurrent state of alarm over proofs. Aeons seemed to pass before the first galleys arrived, and then, so difficult and eccentric was the text, and so unequivocal Bollingen's desire to convey as fully and meticulously as print could, what

Coleridge's intention were, so many strange situations cropped up
in every ten lines of type, that it was necessary to have revised
galleys, page-proofs and revised page-proofs. 1955 and 1956 were
years of galley-slavery. The really alarming consequence of such
generosity in multiple proofs is that the more the revises, the more
the chances of errors creeping in. With a stab of fright one sees in
the final page-proof, 'Cristabel' for 'Christabel', which has been
correct up to then, or still more horrific, in a list of works projected
by Coleridge, by the printer's transposition of a letter, 'An Essay
on Bowles' has become 'An Essay on Bowels', an all too possible
subject for Coleridge in hypochondriacal mood. Most hair-raising
of all the proof-corrections was one that occurred during a September gale on Georgian Bay. After a hectic summer abroad, digging
for Volume 2, I had taken with me the revised page-proofs of
Volume 1 up to B 578 for one more read-through, with no real
expectation of any further corrections whatever. I discovered that
a whole stanza of a two-verse poem had been dropped out. It had
been in the last galleys, but in the cutting up of galleys into pages
it had got lost. How it did so, and how it escaped notice until the
eleventh hour is one of those inexplicable hazards of book production, but there it was, confronting me one stormy September
day on the island. Pages cannot be stretched to accommodate extra
stanzas of verse. I already knew that Bollingen expected the whole
volume to be 'put to bed' the next week, so the absolute deadline
was upon us. Suddenly I saw how the error could be patched up.
Measuring the space with shaking hands, I found that by the incredible good luck of short lines, two stanzas could just be fitted in
opposite each other instead of following one another—a minimal
alteration of our usual style, with no disturbance of the length of
the page. But it had to reach New York in time!

I had no motor boat, and almost all the neighbouring cottages
within five miles or so were closed for the season. One family about
four miles away was pulling out the next day for Cleveland, Ohio.

Leaving a note for Johnson to follow me if he happened to turn
up (because the wind was rising and I was not sure how it would be
on my return trip), and putting three or four sizeable rocks in the
canoe, I tied up the corrected page of proof and a letter in a water-
proof bag and had an exhilarating paddle over a stretch of open
water in a gusting south-wester. The canoe responded as it had

been doing for over twenty years. The Clevelanders were just about to leave, and kindly took my packet and a telephone message to Bollingen. Some years later when someone in England asked—a shade superciliously I thought—if it was true that in Canada the notebooks had to travel by canoe and dog-train, my answer was, 'not by dog-train. Not yet.'

The years of the proofs were also prime for the Index. As it was the first indexing of the notebooks, and therefore would set a pattern for the five volumes, decisions were legion, and crucial, and because of my inexperience, they had to be made and re-made. The patience of my doughty little indexer was often stretched but never exhausted, and she gave that kind of stern support that only a conscientious indexer can give, correcting my errors or laziness, insisting on decisions when I thought I was too busy to make them, and generally sparing neither herself nor me in the interests of her 'Mr Coleridge'. I remember the June night in 1956 when over the telephone in the late hours we realized that the printer's copy of the index must be marked by us to indicate that certain classes of numerals had to be printed in a special fount of type. We decided to put a tick against these figures—a considerable task in an index that eventually in print ran to a hundred and thirty pages. Next morning Gertrude was up at 5 a.m. 'ticking'. When I left at 10.30 a.m. to catch a plane for London she was, she said, 'still ticking'. A pint-size stalwart, at the time of writing this chapter she was a spritely eighty-eight-year-old, still ticking cheerfully, an encouragement to all her friends. The ticking is now silenced; the encouragement remains.

I went to England to check on a few residual small points in the proofs of Volume 1, and to work on Volume 2, to see Jessie Coleridge, and to have talks with Rupert Hart-Davis about the idea of a collected edition of Coleridge's complete works.

First to see Lady Coleridge, now the Dowager Lady Coleridge as she kept reminding me. I longed to see her, and I wanted to consult her wishes about the form of dedication of the *Notebooks* to Geoffrey and herself. Characteristically she thought she should be left out, but when I teased her about how she had put me up to borrowing Notebook 25 and thus started the whole ball rolling, and reminded her of her gentle little managing ways all along the line, she gave in, clearly pleased. 'But, dear Bookie, I never in my wildest dreams thought to see this stupid old frumpish trout connected in print with the brilliant old poet.'

Barbara Rooke—in London from Jamaica to work on *The Friend*, and beloved by the Coleridges—joined forces with me in driving down to Perranporth where Lady Coleridge was staying in Sully's Hotel with her sister. We had hired a car in Exeter, for our plan was to spend two or three days in Perranporth and then to take our dear old Female Frump on a little jaunt down to Land's End, St Michael's Mount, or wherever she wanted to go. It was touching to see her. There she was, not very comfortable in quarters that must have felt painfully cramped after the Chanter's House, perhaps over-economizing (she was always stingy with herself) but being very much our old hostess—with the biscuit jar and the little nose-gay on the bedside table, and the hot-water bottles in the beds. She was thin, and worn, and very sad about some things, as she one day confided. Nevertheless, with a great mixture of sunshine and showers we had a few poignantly beautiful and very happy days. Every parting is a little death, and that one, as her eyes and mine filled with tears when we said good-bye, was more than a little one.

The return journey was a Coleridge family tour, with side-trips to the three great-great-grandsons of STC, all in Devon where Coleridges should be, all hospitable and kind. I always enjoyed these family visits, with lots of gossipy talk about Coleridges living and dead, all very natural and only slightly conveying the impression that none but curious trans-Atlantic freaks like ourselves would be at so much trouble about their famous ancestor, but nevertheless taking a benign interest in our activities and really prouder of the name than decent English family reserve permitted them to show.

We talked again of the possibility of a collected edition, and on the return to London Rupert Hart-Davis and I had more conversations about it. Rupert when the war was over had founded his own publishing firm. I remember a shipboard conversation in which I referred to him as 'one of the best of the young new publishers', at which someone indignantly piped up, 'What do you mean, *one* of the best! He *is* the best.' He and I had been having vague pipe dreams for two or three years about remedying the appallingly neglected state of Coleridge's work, much of it either not published at all or published badly in the mid-nineteenth century. Now we could be more specific. He had had two or three manuscripts of edited Coleridge works offered to him, and we began to talk about editorial principles. Of editors I already had a potential list. The problem was, what American publishing house would help bear the risk? By the time the summer was over we had a clearly thought-out plan to present—to whom?

But for now it was mainly back to the struggle with the Note-books Volume 2. Work on them was becoming a bit more systematic. The paths were now beaten a little and there were fewer blind alleys. Some pitfalls were known. Volume 2, it seemed, could take in the period from Coleridge's departure from the Lakes for Malta in January 1804, to his return to England in August 1806, and probably to early 1808. Though decisions about where these entries began and ended in some of the larger notebooks—those notebooks used both before and after this journey—raised difficult problems, still it was a relatively defined period.

The content was as always a delight to work on, and as always full of problems—such an entry as one now designated 2744, describing a journey in Calabria. Did he make this tour or did he take notes from someone? Was a political mission involved? The search was long and complex and unsuccessful.

Or, to take another sort of problem, what kind of language is Morlack? Coleridge transcribed fourteen lines of Morlack verse in an entry mainly on metres. It comes from Dalmatia, and he extracted his metrical example from the *Travels* of the Abbé Fortis, a distinguished Italian geologist interested in fossil-bones. Though Fortis's work was translated into English (and German) all the evidence shows that Coleridge was reading the Italian edition, where the Morlack lines and an Italian version are on facing pages. Yet he copied out the Morlack into his notebook, being interested in the metre. At first glance, a frightening entry.

'The Morlack Songs as given by Abbé Fortis are endecasyllables, sometimes; but decaysll.—regularly, all trochaics.

Kadlimuje ranam boglie bilo
Ter poruça vjernoi Gliabi svojoi
Ne çe kaime u dvoru bjelomu
Ni u dvoru, ni u rodu momu . . .'

[171]

A helpful member of the Museum staff translated the Morlack lines for me.

> 'As he was suffering from his wounds
> And he sent a message to his faithful wife:
> Do not wail for me in the white palace,
> Neither in the palace, nor among my kinsmen.'

The excerpt of the poem continued:

> 'When the Lady understood [this] speech
> She became even more miserable at the thought.
> The sound of a horse stopped by the palace:
> And Asan-Agha's wife fled
> To break her neck [by throwing herself] down from the
> window of the tower.
>
> . . .
>
> Lest my poor heart should break
> Beholding my orphan girls [her daughters by Asan-Agha]—
> But when they were [going] past Agha's palace
> Her two daughters were looking out of the window.
> And her sons came out before her,
> And remonstrated with their mother.'

In a thousand ways the British Museum staff has always brought its extraordinarily various knowledge to bear incisively on my thousands of curious Coleridge questions. I think I only ever had one rude rebuff, and that one was so ridiculous I have treasured it. It arose out of investigations in connexion with a simple-looking entry:

> 'What was the Price of Corn in the first year of *Sir A.B.'s* Administ / the second? the third?—And what have been the prices in the corresponding Years in Italy and Sicily?'

The price of wheat, as I explain in my note to the entry, was the crucial question for the economy of both Malta and Sicily in 1805. It was crucial also in a political controversy over Alexander Ball's administration as British High Commissioner, when private (and foreign?) interests were trying to discredit him and to restore the corn-buying to private interests rather than the government agents he recommended. In Sicily the grain trade was in the hands of a monopoly, the main cause of poverty there. Coleridge was keenly aware of the whole problem, and as Ball's private secretary was at one time to go to the Black Sea on a wheat-buying mission in Russia.

Wishing to get to the bottom of the political gossip and the wire-pulling, I ordered in the British Museum a volume in which Ball was attacked by an enemy, William Eton, *Authentic Materials for a History of the People of Malta*. It was, I suppose, not strictly necessary to an understanding of Coleridge's memorandum, but one keeps on turning over stones, not knowing. The little volume bore two book-plates, some sort of royal one covering another underneath it. I needed to know whose they were, and particularly whose was the one underneath, a clue to the first owner. If it had been the Earl of Camden, Colonial Secretary at the time, or Lord Harrowby, the Foreign Secretary, it might be interesting to find Eton's influence against Ball in high places. I therefore asked through the officials in the North Library if the top book-plate could be floated off. The following reply came on a torn-off piece of scrap paper:

'The bookplate underneath is identical, except for the press-mark, with the bookplate which had been superimposed on top of it.

Royal dukes do not generally buy secondhand books.'

I refrained from several obvious replies. The snobbish silliness was a marked exception to the usual attitude in the British Museum. It also indicates how far from poetry and philosophy one's Coleridge researches may lead one.

1956 ended with no sight of page-proofs of the first volume, but it also ended with a British Council invitation to teach for six weeks in Jamaica—an unexpected sunny winter interlude. I remember leaving Toronto airport on the morning of December 16th, the thermometer at exactly zero Fahrenheit, and arriving in Kingston Jamaica at 85 degrees. Almost the first sound I heard was young Caribbean voices singing,

'Jingle bells, jingle bells, jingle all the way,
O what fun it is to ride in a one-horse open sleigh . . .'

When I asked some students next day about the song, and where they learned it, I found they hadn't the faintest idea what a one-horse open sleigh was; somehow they felt it belonged to the Christmas season.

The students were a great pleasure, though, because of the arrangement of courses and the combining of classes, it was not always easy to know what they had worked on and could be expected to know. The cross-currents were amusing—George Eliot and *Middlemarch* with questions about Ben Jonson and *Volpone* interspersed. A Coleridge seminar could lead to Kant, the slave trade, Milton's sonnets and Wordsworth's, local politics . . . in fact to almost anything. These young people were not so passive mentally as their shy behaviour at times suggested. I recall a public evening lecture to about sixty people, all very polite and too proper, with faculty having to think up the questions and students making the most discerning remarks afterwards. I think I gave them a fairly stiff shot on why Coleridge is worth the trouble of editing.

But term there was nearly over and Jamaica was more play than work, good times with individual students and various hospitable faculty members. Some especially lively arguments I remember with Hugh Springer. We disagreed about whether Eden should have resigned over Suez, and time, from that argument onwards, has strengthened our friendship. There was a memorable country drive with wise old Philip Sherlock, who knew everyone we met, took us to see people in their homes as well as in Father Cheyney's school at Above Rocks, and who, as we returned through the tropical dark, stopped and bought the hottest and best meat pasties I have ever tasted.

For my own archives of Coleridge experience, the richest deodand there was the tropical night, for there indeed, 'At one stride comes the dark'. The poetic miracle was also actual flesh-stabbing truth. Never more so than on the night of the students' Christmas dinner. Against the high white walls moved the dark skins and scarlet St Andrews gowns of the students, the white jackets of waiters and waitresses threading in and out, the flickerings of candle flame and of lavish poinsettias as the motion of the air stirred them; and outside the open windows glowed the night sky, velvet-black and full of big stars.

Jamaica preceded a rough wintry spring. Graduate students seemed particularly demanding, on the doorstep at all hours of the night. My mother was ill with a painfull illness that required a good deal of attention. There were flurries about index decisions, made and countermanded, and long telephone calls to New York. Where were the revised page-proofs? Delays, delays, delays. No sign of the pages of the index proofs. Why not? Publication had been predicted for 1956. Now it seemed as if no date mattered.

I went to Chicago in April to give a lecture or two on an exchange scheme Toronto had with Chicago, Cornell and Western Reserve. The highlight of that expedition was a good visit with Cecil Bald, and a glimpse of what he was doing with all the John Donne materials he had lovingly collected. He respected Coleridge, having laboured over transcribing some notebooks in 1934. 'Thicker than raindrops on November thorn,' I reminded him, as we passed a leafless drizzle-laden shrub. His face saddened. 'Alas, I am so far away from Coleridge now,' he said. But he was not too far away to give a lively dinner party two or three years later, at which a good hock Coleridge mentioned was drunk and shooting arrows with cross-bows into a neighbouring field was the main entertainment, endangering the lives of some good cattle until we lost most of the arrows.

But on the return from Chicago there came hard news. Jessie Coleridge died in her sleep on April 25th, 1957. Three days after the cable came from Richard Lord Coleridge, I had from her a postcard she had posted by sea mail ten days earlier. The black and white photograph was of a small one-man dinghy, empty, lonely, floating sheltered under a willow tree in the quiet backwater of an inland stream. A few days later, even more of a shock, another card arrived from her, written a day or two before she slipped away. The indefatigable postcard-sender to the end! This time it was a picture of the simple stone Cobb at Lyme Regis, looking out from the Dorset coast towards a bright shining horizon, over a 'wide wide sea'. No shelter now. 'Frumpy Trout', as she signed herself on these cards, was gone, gone without warning 'into the world of light'. It was as she wished.

There were still index-proofs for Volume 1, and ahead a summer of steady writing of Notes for Volume 2. As the exactingness of the concentration became clearly more demanding, I decided to build myself a separate working cabin on B578. So Jessie Macpherson and I drove up in June, my friend John Hall came and drew the plan, and in July the cabin was built, a great addition. That summer it was particularly desirable to draft as many Notes as possible for Volume 2, before September, in order to be aware of the gaps that needed to be plugged by library work in the next year. Guggenheim had renewed my Fellowship and I planned to visit the American collections of Coleridgiana in the autumn. Perhaps I was really just hovering about New York, waiting for the production of Volume 1 rather like a pregnant mother close to her time.

At last it came, 5th of November, Guy Fawkes day, 1957, not a highly propitious date. The first pleasure was turning pages instead of flapping ungainly galleys or pages of typescript. Of the reception of that first volume I remember little. As the saying is, it exceeded all expectations. But that was because I had formed no expectations as to any public response. I knew it was a job worth doing. The work itself was enough reward; I was now more worried about Volume 2. That other people found the *Notebooks* interesting, even exciting, was an extra. The review that most annoyed me was one that coyly suggested that my notes were more interesting than the text. Rubbish. Not, I felt, either good sense, good taste, nor any compliment to my judgment. But on the whole the reviews would have been a spur to Volume 2 had one been needed.

The most rewarding consequence of all, though it was not apparent for a year or more, was that Bollingen was gratified, and perhaps so surprised by the extent of the reception of that first volume of the *Notebooks*, that it eventually agreed to sponsor an edition of Coleridge's collected works, the twenty-five or so volumes of the plan Rupert Hart-Davis and I had drawn in outline.

That 1957–8 English winter was pleasantly sociable; yet I was engrossed mentally in 1804–1806. Towards the end of that period, Coleridge has been reading some strange Irish books, or books about Irish affairs, some of which I could not track down in England. For one thing, I needed to know whether their publication dates, or something of the contents, would be decisive in assigning notebook entries from them to my Volume 2 or to Volume 3. Armed with an introduction from my old Toronto friend, now in

Oxford, Herbert Davis, the editor of Swift, to James Haynes, the chief Librarian of the National Library of Ireland, and to Sean White, the editor of *Irish Writing*, I made a spring journey in 1958 to Dublin. Sean White, gave me a beautiful day-long tour of Joyce's Dublin, and Joyce's pubs, ending up with a dinner, memorable for talk and a splendid pepper steak. As I entertained him and a university teacher of the Irish language, plying them with questions, listening to their half-cheerful, half-grousing conversation, the very temper and spirit of Joyce seemed alive and present—with here and there a shaft of Swift, too.

The National Librarian was a composed, pleasant gentleman in grey Irish tweed, imperturbable, crinkly-eyed, who, having turned on all the courtesies of the library, settled in for a bit of chat. Somehow the talk got round to indexing and the need for better indexes.

'We have here a complete file of the oldest daily paper in the English language,' he said, 'and I am having it indexed—*for free!*' The astonishment and the questions he intended to solicit were easily forthcoming.

'Well,' he said, 'one morning I had an inspiration. In the morning paper I read the police-court news of a forger getting two or three years, and so I just picked up that telephone there and called the superintendent of the penitentiary. "How many forgers, embezzlers, and other bright boys have you got with good long terms? I'm not interested in anybody with less than two years," I said. So he gave me six chaps, put them in a workroom by themselves, and we sent over a librarian for a few days, with some filing cards. One of the six soon became the head indexer, and by Jove, they are doing a good job and enjoying it. They get one extra cigarette a day, and curfew for them is extended by an hour, so they like it. They send their cards back every two weeks now, and they are checked here. They ask for books from the library to help them to understand the subjects they are dealing with—books on architecture, for instance, on government, history—everything. Those chaps are getting some education. And look here,'—he pulled out his library report of the year just past—'I have made acknowledgements to them all, by name—of course without their addresses.'

I tried to interest some prison officials in the idea when I got home, but unsuccessfully.

The National Library answered most of my Coleridge questions, and provided some unexpected little extras as well, some of which appear in my notes. I yearned to stay longer in Dublin, a beautiful, complicated, sad city, but the British Museum was calling insistently.

In June 1958 de la Mare gave up asking his unanswerable questions. There was a huge congregation in St Paul's Cathedral, where he had sung as a choirboy, to bid the traveller farewell. I never saw so many distinguished tears unconcealed. It was a particularly moving service because one knew from many of the poems and from many of his questions that thoughts of death were never far from the surface of his mind. I remembered what was perhaps our best and freest talk one day when we were alone together. He had heard I owned an island and asked scores of questions about it. It appeared to me that death, for him, was a kind of island, or that an island was a kind of death, a way of cheating death perhaps. He asked me what I should do if I ever found myself dumped out of a plane in an unknown country—alone—at night.

'Curl up under a tree and go to sleep,' I said.

'What a wonderful thing to be able to say! Would you really sleep?'

'I hope so. Why not? Better be ready for the morning?' He shook his head.

On an earlier visit in 1952 he had dated his inscription in my copy of *Winged Chariot*, 'August 1942'. His Freudian slip gave him away. I thought of Coleridge, accusing himself of failure to keep up with time's winged chariot, and of making himself out to be a year and a day guiltily older than in fact he was; WJ, fear-haunted, unconsciously longing to put a finger on the spoke of Time's wheel, had wished himself ten years younger. But now,

'Last of all last words spoken is, Good-bye.'

The winter of 1958–9 in Toronto was full of teaching and writing notes, notes, notes. It was a good feasting time, but the spring was darkened by serious illnesses in the family. So it was an immense relief in June 1959 to go off to Saskatoon to the meetings of the Royal Society of Canada, and the other learned societies that meet in conjunction with it. As I had always been away in England at such times, and had never been received as a Fellow, and as George Whalley was being received also, it was a good year to go. Though we gave no papers that year, we did cause the name of Coleridge to be pronounced a few times. I enjoyed those meetings. Perhaps they are not always so good as that first time, but there were lively intellectual exchanges combined with pleasanter, more gentle, more humane attitudes than sometimes obtain in academic circles. I was proud of it. And the setting was lovely—the spacious green campus with the buildings almost all of warm yellowish sandstone, which, I noted with pleasure, was being hewn and laid on the spot. The university community was young, spirited, eager for the future, enthusiastic about the transformations they were making under their own eyes every day.

On that trip I went for the first time to the west coast, and on Vancouver Island did a little non-Coleridgian research for another sort of pleasure. Emily Carr, a painter of considerable power, had owned a house in Victoria, British Columbia, which late in life she she maintained as a boarding house, her studio being on the top floor. This was a miserable time for her, described in her book, *The House of All Sorts*. She used to retreat to a low attic, her bedroom, and paint on the sloping rafters of the ceiling, 'Indian eagles, to make strong talk for me'. I wanted to find that house, and those eagles, and I had a very few hours in which to do it. After two or three wrong doorbells, I found the house. The lady who opened the door was somewhat staggered by my request to see her attic. 'But,' she said, 'how do you know about those eagles? I haven't owned this house very long and we only discovered them a month ago!' I explained, and discovered behind a dour exterior another Emily Carr enthusiast. 'How good are you on a ladder?' she said darkly. The room had been boarded up, and a ladder to the floor of it through a small opening was the only entrance. Carrying up the ladder from the garden, and mounting—and again in a sprawling position rather like the dive for the Philosophical Lectures in the Reverend Mr Gerard Coleridge's study—I saw! Not just eagles, though they did indeed 'make strong talk', but between each eagle and the next an Indian infant, painted red. Poor dear Klee Wyck (the Laughing One, as her Indian friends called her), how she had longed to give love! There it was, utterly spelled out—her babies—

in the thick of all the strong talk. Coleridge's Christmas carol described her:

> 'And closer still the Babe she pressed;
> And while she cried, the Babe is mine!
> The milk rushed faster to her breast:
> Joy rose within her like a summer's morn.'

He has many references to the babe at the breast.

> 'It would have made the loving mother dream
> That she was softly bending down to kiss
> Her babe, that something more than babe did seem . . .'

he wrote in *The Day Dream*.

On returning to Toronto I found a pristine copy of I. A. Richards's *Coleridge on Imagination* on my desk. Dining with the Richardses and Norrie and Helen Frye in London one evening on my last trip, I had found myself agreeing to a preposterous proposition. I.A. said that I once spoke kindly of his book *Coleridge on Imagination*, but had added that there were a few things I couldn't agree with. Would I annotate a copy he would send me, blackening the margins with my objections? He was going to do a third edition. Norrie threw me a compassionate 'How do you get out of that?' sort of look, but I knew I should have to do as I was bidden—some day. With a struggle against being quite unnerved by it, and yet enjoying it, I tackled the task in the summer of '59 and had a few notes ready when Richards came to Toronto to give a lecture. When I met him at the station his first remark was, 'Now I hope we are going to have a good chunk of time to chew our way through this thing—if you can spare it.'

So most of Sunday we 'chewed', a great mixture of intense pleasure and soul-wracking temerity on my part, all made great fun by Ivor's gaiety and giggles. I remember saying, 'I don't understand the meaning of that sentence' and his answer 'I don't understand what I meant either! I suppose it meant something at the time.'

Or about another bit: 'You don't believe that any more.'

I.A.R. 'No. I suppose I don't. You're right—no—certainly not.

Shall I cut out that whole last section there?'

'No. It's partial truth, and it's good to see how you've arrived where you are. Haven't you been converted by your subject?' And on it went, with all unimaginable cheekiness.

He had given friends my telephone number and the thing in the next room rang constantly. Every time he left to go to the telephone he flung a paper at me out of one pocket or another. 'Read that in the meantime,' he said, and after about the third fling of the kind, 'I am going to publish a little volume of my poems.' It was the first I had heard of poems. They became *Goodbye Earth*. Something in our talk about them led to the subject of Georgian Bay, though I fear not much of a lead was necessary. He understood and expressed better than anyone ever had my occasional need and enjoyment of being alone on the island, and the folly of other people's fears for one's safety. 'One develops in such situations a self-protective caution,' he said. And we agreed eye to eye that life was not to either of us worth living on any other terms.

A few months later—or was it weeks?—there came an apologetic letter from him. After all, the third edition of *Coleridge on Imagination* was to be done by offset, a paperback, with no possibility of changes in the text. Instead, what he had wrung from his publisher was permission for a new foreword. Could I perhaps sum up my objections and generalize them enough to write such a piece? It struck me as so like Richards, and highly Coleridgian, to suggest that his book should be back-handedly introduced to a reader by an essay, 'Why I disagree with this book', that I accepted the challenge, and the compliment. After all, when STC was campaigning for support for *The Watchman*, his newspaper, had he not entertained a company with a powerful condemnation of all newspapers and newspaper-reading?

'But not till summer,' I said, 'on the island.'

It was the most difficult assignment I had ever undertaken, but over it hovered the fun and candour of our wonderful Sunday, and therefore it was done with all the *joie de vivre* that Richards brings to everything. Trying to make my way through the occasionally choppy waters of Richards in *Coleridge on Imagination* was at times like paddling a canoe without enough weight in the bow against a head-wind three-quarters on. I felt, in short, a little light for the run, but the muscle-toning exercise was glorious.

XI

1959–1960

Towards the end of that summer of 1959, work on Volume 2 being virtually completed, I meditated a little on the whole experience of editing Coleridge.

Could I have endured him in the flesh? As a person he could be childish, irritating, even infuriating; he could also be wise, extraordinarily sensitive, gently sympathetic, and charming. As well as being full of zest, generosity, and intelligent awareness of those around him, he could be jealous, self-pitying and sometimes disgustingly obsequious. In short this great man, who endeared himself to so many and had a broad and profound influence on his time, was full of personal miseries and unheroic weaknesses. But in the end there was always a certain magnitude of mind, if not always of emotion, though often that too. He picked other people's ideas off the trees everywhere—to look at them in the light of his own acute observations, to judge them with originality, and to combine ideas by his own logic so as to confront us with the great issues, of life and thought and belief and creativity. Perhaps as a contemporary I might have shared the Wordsworths' increasing despair and their limited view; now I see it as their loss, their lack. And even at that, Wordsworth said that Coleridge was 'the only wonderful man' he had ever known. Certainly in our own time, now that the fragile creaturely veil is torn away, we can see, unimpeded, his greatness—a courageous, inquiring, inspiring spirit. No other writer so perpetually and so deeply astonishes me.

Polar opposites like Charles Lamb and Frederick Denison Maurice took him for what he was. I have a fear lest I should have been put off by the adenoids, the river of talk, or some other trivial irritant. Who knows? Perhaps there are advantages in being born a century and a half too late. As for the editorial process through which Coleridge puts me, I have long thought that the two best places for it have been the British Museum and Georgian Bay. The

BM is the one and only library for Coleridge work. Not only because it has the largest collection of his manuscripts and annotated books, but because one is surer there than anywhere else of being able to find the precise edition of any work to which Coleridge refers. For so close a reader as he was, this is essential. But why Georgian Bay?

I suppose it is that whereas in other places, in Toronto, in London, any city, the rhythms of life and the rhythm of work are often felt to be in conflict; here on the island, where I am now writing, they seem peculiarly to interact as one harmony, and have been doing so from the beginning and will to the end.

The first and most important part of the process of editing the notebooks was to find out

'. . . by nature's quietness
And solitary musings . . .'

what the questions really were. Later in the British Museum, weeks and months were needed to dig and delve for answers, and to squirrel away hundreds of reference acorns. The third stage, the writing of notes or polishing them to as concentrated a form as possible, seems always again to require the Georgian Bay peace; in any case, by necessity or choice, the wide expanse of fresh water, the granite rock, the insistent presence of the elements, have steadied the perspective when at times the whole undertaking threatened to become overwhelming.

In the beginning, during the wartime summers, the process was a straightforward one of physical ordering, reading, accumulating some sense of STC's interests and chief concerns, not worrying too much about particular last-ditch problems. From Coleridge himself one learned the advantages of trying first to grasp some sense of a whole without being held up by details. Here, overlooking the great sweep of Lake Huron, was the spacious opportunity to try to see the vast wood—taking note, merely, of the trees—to roam freely through the whole magnificent forest of his mind.

This land-and-water-scape is pre-Cambrian; in other words its age is unknown. Before man, before any animals, or any vegetation, it was. It goes back to frost and fire, to the primeval volcano and the ur-glacier. Its granite is the product of upheavings and down-sinkings, and all the convulsive writhings of cosmic chaos. The scores of thousands of rocky islands, falling into the long curved rough lines of old mountain ridges, are the roots that alone survived the grinding and pounding of primordial storms. In wartime, as one looked at or lay on its smooth glacier-carved contours, one could not fail to think piteously of the frailty of the world's cities being levelled to dust and of the ephemeral existence of man. Some parts of the Bay have limestone shores or sandy beaches; here we live on granite—feldspar, quartz and mica, with seams of black basalt—rock that once miraculously bore great forests. In the nineteenth century, by ignorant and ruthless timbering, the mainland was nearly denuded of its huge virgin pines and hardwoods; second-growth trees only were left. But on the islands the great white pines growing out of the crevices still stand, huge primeval trees as well as younger ones. Most of the larger animals moved away, but still the occasional bear and fox are seen, the deer in winter cross on the ice, and beavers build their houses still in many a sheltered backwater. A mink usually inhabits B578, leaving his crayfish shells at the water's edge. A night-prowling porcupine will sometimes set about his monotonous munching of the underpinnings of the house. On June nights, the whip-poor-wills carry on their incessant courtships, and, alas, more and more rarely, the great northern loon pierces long distances with his cry; sweetest of all, the white-throat raises his long high liquid trills, ending with 'Can-ada Can-ada Can-ada'.

The great granite masses are a setting for the minuter pleasures too; the many mosses, twin-flower with its two delicate sweet-scented pinkbells on one stem, pipsissewa, spikes of spicy orchises, lady's slippers, violets, the purple and the very tiny sweet white ones, blue irises (reflected in rock pools after rain), wild roses, meadowsweet, and cardinal flower that attracts the humming bird. Fragility nestles in the crevices of the rock. And the great heavy flowers, like the magenta Joe Pye weed, golden rod, and the purple pickerel weed are the glories of late summer.

After most of a lifetime's summers on the Bay—swimming in it, washing one's teeth in it down by the shore, listening to its silences or its fury, recording on one's retinas the rich green-black night waters or the spectacular electric storms that turn the gunmetal wet rocks into hammered silver, one finds it difficult to put into words anything at all that does not seem trivial in the perspective of the total experience.

It is not only the obvious advantages of seclusion—and it is not always secluded, fortunately. It is not *just* the quiet, the absence of the telephone and the daily post, the daily paper and all the time-wasting goings-on of city life. It is all these, and the SPACE. But it is also many things: the familiar branch across a path; the known crevices in the rock; the sense of rootedness in earth and granite; one's active relationship to an immense variety of forms of life that yet have an independent life of their own. The very existence of the island as a fact is a rest, a relief, from oneself, from the personal life, but also deeply re-assuring, year after year. The consciousness every day, sometimes from hour to hour, of the weather; the growth of that little red pine since last year; the everlasting crickets from June onwards; the evening primrose at the back doorstep—will some clumsy foot crush it? The water, low this year, exposing new contours at the shore; the splendid old dead pine, still standing. It is also the feeling, when one goes up at the beginning of summer, that the heavy, sedentary body, clumsy on the rocks, tired, slow, creaking, gives way, gradually, to some elasticity—the lighter leaps from rock to rock, the leathery feel of the waist muscles as the axe or the paddle swings more freely and smoothly. In short the gradual but perceptible changes from a sodden town blob to a more or less controlled body are enforced by this landscape. And the swimming! Cold at first, even icy—a quick dart in and out—the daily toughening and longer swims as the water warms up under the sun. And there is the old green canoe, experienced traveller of many hundreds of miles. Quieter and more sinuous than the first skating in winter is the first dip of a paddle after many months of absence, and the soft pace of the canoe with you. It is like falling into step beside a friend long absent with whom one has no need to resume conversation.

One thing is puzzling—partly—the thoughts of friends who have never been here. The bay is a strong bond among those who know it really well, and there has been the great happiness of sensitive and civilized companionship. But why is Jessie Coleridge here too —why associated with the swimming bay? Perhaps just because with her affectionate, perceptive questions she entered into so many of one's pleasures. And of those who have been here, one is aware constantly of Jessie Mac, whose brown bread and witty self-persiflage and intellectual hardihood still nourish us, though now only in memory; and of Edith Buchanan, one of the oldest school friends, now in India, undoubtedly thinking at times, even though she has the Himalayas to look at, of Georgian Bay. And Sam Zacks, our most ardent fisherman, ardent about everything, whose exploits with black bass are a part of our life, though he will never proudly bring in another catch. There is here a mental and temporal space in which the mind roams back and forth. The past, a very long past as well as the shorter human past, is here, and good for Coleridge thoughts. How he would have noted the extremes meeting!

Without this Georgian Bay Island B578 and its special ordering of life, the progress of the ordering of the Notebooks on paper and of the clarifying of Coleridgian ideas in my mind would have been slower, poorer, altogether less rewarding than it has been. The island has been the imperturbable untangler of tangled skeins, the silent weaver of the work. Other factors, other helpers have contributed their invaluable shares, but without the energy-giving peace and harmony of the Bay, the work would seem less a whole, and would contain more errors than it does. STC on Georgian Bay has had reprieves that STC in Keswick was denied, reprieves from the tensions that paralyse and obstruct. Here has been the absence of pressure and the presence of affirmation.

England provided the manuscripts and Coleridge himself, and the Coleridge family, who variously have participated and co-operated. It provided the whole cultural tradition out of which he came and which interested and excited me. Then New York and the Bollingen Foundation provided assistance of every kind, in the pursuits of research and in the publication of the *Notebooks*. They provided funds, but also that without which the funds would have amounted to much less—enthusiastic understanding, trust, and good taste.

By 1959 or even earlier, we were all on both sides of the Atlantic, talking about going beyond the *Notebooks* to the first complete edition of all the Works, those printed and those still in manuscript, for some of the more important things were still unknown. Among ourselves we called it 'the Susquehanna Scheme', touching our caps to that abortive plan of Southey and Coleridge, as young men in 1794, to establish an ideal literary community on the banks of the Susquehanna River, an American land agent having persuaded them that 'literary men make money there'. We were more realistic but we had the pleasant sense of somehow bringing something of another kind to fruition. By June 1960 the general plan for producing the Collected Coleridge, had been worked out by Rupert Hart-Davis and the Bollingen Foundation. They announced it in *The Times Literary Supplement* for 1 July (Dominion Day to Canadians, and my parents' wedding day), 1960:

The First Complete Edition
of the Works of
S. T. COLERIDGE
will be published jointly by
RUPERT HART-DAVIS LTD
in London, and the
BOLLINGEN FOUNDATION
Under the general editorialship of
in New York
KATHLEEN COBURN
Victoria College
University of Toronto
The edition will consist of about twenty volumes,
including an index volume. The first will appear
in 1961. Details about prices and dates of
publication will be given in due course.

There followed the list of titles and editors. Five editors were English, four Americans, two Australians, and three Canadians. The first volume to appear was *The Friend*. There have naturally and sadly been some changes since the announcement of 1960, but the *Collected Coleridge*, as we have come to call it, is another story, still in the telling.* The announcement of it marked a new fork in the Coleridge road.

---

* At this time of writing, early in 1977, six volumes have been published, representing seven of the sixteen titles announced. Of the *Notebooks*, a separate work in five double volumes, three double volumes have been published—Text and Notes—comprising some four thousand five hundred entries.

EPILOGUE

On the sixth of June 1961 Coleridge was re-buried in Highgate Parish Church and a memorial service was held which someone described as the most cheerful, the most triumphant funeral he had ever attended.

About three years earlier Ernest Raymond, the novelist, had written a letter to *The Times*, denouncing the neglect of Coleridge's tomb in Highgate. As correspondence mounted I could see that the family was going to come in for criticism. The Borough Council and the Parochial Church Council were arguing as to the responsibility for the property on which the tomb stood. I wrote to Alwyne Coleridge, begging the family to take some initiative before the affair should become acrimonious. He replied with one of his more amusing letters, telling me that Mrs STC had thought the tomb a great waste of money, a needless extravagance, that there was one empty place in it (the bodies of STC and Mrs STC, their daughter, Sara, and her husband, Henry Nelson Coleridge, and their son, Herbert being there) and he thought that as in life I had been so associated with STC's works, perhaps in death I would like 'to be placed in close proximity to his mortal remains'. As he, Alwyne, had the key to the vault, he offered to present me with it. 'Nearer the time, naturally, of your demise!' I think I replied that I shouldn't be in a very good position to unlock it then. In due course Raymond's letter, supported by John Masefield, John Betjeman, Richard Church, Cecil Day-Lewis, Christopher Fry, J.E.Morpurgo (Director, National Book League), Harold Nicolson, Kathleen Raine, Louis A.Arabin (Mayor of St Pancras), Bernard Waley-Cohen (Lord Mayor of London), succeeded in raising a fund and a new grave was made for Coleridge in St Michael's and All Angels, Highgate, where the interment and the cheerful memorial service took place.

Dear 'Uncle Walter' (the late W.H.P.Coleridge, a great-grandson) wrote the best account of it I received, and as it says something about STC's persistent life, I quote it in part.

'. . . I expect you have heard from Ernest Raymond all about the

great day. I do wish you could have been present. The Church
was packed. There must have been at least 1000 people present
as it is a big church with balcony. A Grecian from Christ's
Hospital read the 1st lesson & Tony [his nephew and STC's
great great grandson, the Reverend A.D.Coleridge] the 2nd.
The Bishop of London dedicated the tomb. The slab on top of
the tomb which is of course below the floor of the nave is made
of Cumberland slate—a beautiful shade of green and the lettering
cut by Reynolds Stone is very lovely. He is the leading artist in
that line in Britain and has done memorials in Eton College
Chapel & St Pauls & the Abbey. John Masefield gave a very fine
address—a bit long I thought and of course I knew it all before
but I expect very few of the congregation did.

There was a large contingent of Coleridges and direct descendants present. Lady Coleridge was there but Lord C. could not
come. Lady Cave was there too—I expect you know her.

After the service Sir Mark & Lady Turner gave a reception at
No 3 the Grove which I thought was very kind of them. About
a hundred or more people were there and most of us made a
pilgrimage to STC's room—it still has the same old bookcases . . .

In case you have not had one I am sending you a copy of the
service paper.'

So there they all were on that gloriously sunny June day, in the
Church of St Michael's and All Angels beautifully decorated with
a profusion of white flowers packed in to the roof to honour old
STC. The Mayor was there, and—did they sit side by side?—the
Master of Jesus College Cambridge and the Colonel of The 15th
Light Dragoons, to which as a troubled undergraduate Coleridge
fled and enlisted? Two choirs sang, one of them from the local
school—children were much a part of his life in the Grove. The
frail, white-haired Poet Laureate of 1961 was there, as the Poet
Laureate of 1834 had not been. The Ottery relations were also
there, drawn to visit 'Uncle Sam' as they ocasionally had done in
life—in spite of his being 'a bit of a blot' on the family escutcheon.
Many distinguished Americans found their way to Highgate, as
they also had done in his time. More than a thousand persons,
young and old, rich and poor, learned and simple, trudged up
Highgate Hill to share in Highgate's pride.

EPILOGUE

The Lesson that was read by the Christ's Hospital Grecian was from Ecclesiasticus 44, the traditional Speech Day Lesson of Christ's Hospital. Even under the strong emotions flowing out to every familiar word, some persons present must have had, intermittently, a few bitter-sweet recollections of some of Coleridge's own more deprecatory phrases.

Let us now praise famous men, and our fathers that begat us.
The Lord hath wrought great glory by them . . .

> 'I have a sense of power without strength . . .'
> 'Work without Hope draws nectar in a sieve
> And Hope without an object cannot live.'

. . . And by their knowledge of learning meet for the people, wise and eloquent in their instructions: Such as found out musical tunes and recited verses in writing . . .

> 'Ah! silly Bard, . . .
> With scarce a penny in his pocket
> Nay—tho' he hid it from the many—
> With scarce a pocket for his penny!'

. . . There be of them that have left a name behind them, that their praises might be reported . . .

> 'Imagination, honourable aims;
> Free converse with the choir that cannot die;
> Science and song, delight in little things . . .'

The people will tell of their wisdom, and the congregation will show forth their praise.

The congregation sang,

> 'Who would true valour see
> Let him come hither . . .', the Pilgrim hymn.

And as one might have anticipated, an anthem was composed for the occasion on the words from *The Rime of the Ancient Mariner*,

> 'He prayeth well, who loveth well
> Both man and bird and beast.
> He prayeth best, who loveth best
> All things both great and small;

For the dear God who loveth us,
He made and loveth all.'

And then, after the address, they filed past the simple piece of green Cumberland slate, each inwardly no doubt, after his fashion, laying his laurel upon it.

Beneath this stone lies the body of
SAMUEL TAYLOR
COLERIDGE
Born 21 October 1772. Died 25 July 1834.
Stop, Christian passer-by! Stop, child of God,
And read with gentle breast. Beneath this sod
A poet lies, or that which once seem'd he.
O lift one thought in prayer for S.T.C.;
That he who many a year with toil of breath
Found death in life, may here find life in death!
Mercy for praise—to be forgiven for fame
He ask'd, and hoped, through Christ.
Do thou the same!

As I read the service and the many letters about it, both giving the sense that we were rediscovering Coleridge in our generation, I thought of something written in his notebook when he was about thirty-five years old, and, trapped in conflict between a sense of his powers and a terrible sense of his weaknesses, he was thinking about posterity.

'Not only Chaucer and Spenser, but even Shakespere and Milton have as yet received only the earnest, and scanty first gatherings of their Fame—This indeed it is which gives its full dignity and more than mental grandeur to Fame, . . . that it grows with the growth of virtue and intellect and co-operates in that growth; it becomes wider and deeper, as their country and all mankind are the countrymen of the man of true and adequately exerted Genius.'

'Adequately exerted Genius?' some may ask. Again his own valiant word:
'By what I *have* done am I to be judged. What I might have done is a matter for my own conscience.'

Nicholas Coleridge

John = Sarah Ealeb
1678-1730 | d.1705

John = Mary Wills
1697-1739 | 1698-1776

| John | Mary = John Tucker | William | Elizabeth = Samuel |
| 1715-1716 | 1717-1793 | b. & d 1721 | b.1723 Mudge |

Mary Lendon (1) = John = (2) Ann Bowden
1719-1781 | 1727-1809
Vicar and
Master of
King's School

James = Frances   Edward   George = Jane Hart
1796-1836 | Duke Taylor   1760-1843   1764-1828
"The | 1759-1838   Vicar of   Master of
Colonel" | co-heiress   Buckerell   King's School

George May
1798-1847
dsp

James Duke   John Taylor = Mary   Francis George = Harriet
D.C.L. | 1790-1876 Buchanan   1794-1854 | Norris
1789-1857 | The   Arthur Duke
Judge   1830-1913

Mary Elizabeth (poet)
1861-1907

John Duke = (1) Jane Fortescue   Henry James, D.D.
(Baron) Coleridge | Seymour   1822-1893
1820-1894 | 1846   Order of Jesuits
Lord | (2) Amy Lawford   dsp
Chief Justice | 1885
of England

Mildred Mary = C.W. Adams   Bernard John = Mary Alethea
b. 1847   Seymour | Mackarness
1851-1927 | d. 1940
Second Baron

Geoffrey Duke = Jessie Alethea   Audrey Jane   Phillis Mary
1877-1955 | Mackarness   b. 1878   1883-1950
Third Baron | 1880-1957

Richard Duke   John Seymour Duke   Ronald James Duke
1905—   1908—   1911-1972
has issue   had issue

Some members of the Coleridge family

ke =Sarah   Ann   Francis Syndercombe   Samuel Taylor
man| Hart   1769-1791   1770-1792   1772-1834
-1790| India   The poet
    William Hart, D.D.=Sarah   dsp   (See over) ⟶
    1789-1849 | Rennell
Bishop of Barbados |
    had issue

nces =Rt. Hon. Sir John   Henry Nelson =Sara   Edward
ike   Patterson   1798-1843 | Coleridge   1800-1883
6-1842   1802-1852   Fellow of Eton
    had issue
ohn Coleridge Patterson   Herbert   Edith
    1827-1871   1830-1861   1832-1911
Bishop of Melanesia   dsp

ary Frances   Alethea = John Fielder   Frederick William
Keble   Buchanan   Mackarness,   d. 1843
24-1898   b. 1826   Bishop of   dsp
    Oxford

phen William = Geraldine   Gilbert James Duke = Marion
Buchanan | Lushington   1859-1953 | Darroch
1854-1936   had issue
    had issue

Coleridge family (continued)

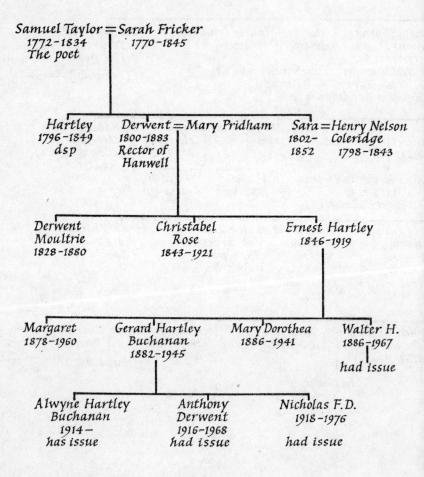

Samuel Taylor = Sarah Fricker
1772-1834   1770-1845
The poet

Hartley   Derwent = Mary Pridham   Sara = Henry Nelson
1796-1849   1800-1883   1802-   Coleridge
dsp   Rector of   1852   1798-1843
                 Hanwell

Derwent   Christabel   Ernest Hartley
Moultrie   Rose   1846-1919
1828-1880   1843-1921

Margaret   Gerard Hartley   Mary Dorothea   Walter H.
1878-1960   Buchanan   1886-1941   1886-1967
                 1882-1945
                                                        had issue

Alwyne Hartley   Anthony   Nicholas F.D.
Buchanan   Derwent   1918-1976
1914-   1916-1968
has issue   had issue   had issue

INDEX